MEMPHIS STATE UNIVERSITY PRESS

This is copy ___469___
of an edition of 2,000 copies
published August, 1979.

Tennessee County History Series

EDITORIAL ADVISORY BOARD

Anderson County,

by Katherine B. Hoskins, 1908-

Joy Bailey Dunn
Editor

Charles W. Crawford
Associate Editor

tc hs

MEMPHIS STATE UNIVERSITY PRESS
Memphis, Tennessee

Designed by Gary G. Gore.

ISBN: 0-87870-061-7

Foreword

The Tennessee County History Series, when completed, will contain more than 13,000 pages of material, much previously unpublished, about the history of our state. It seems appropriate that this unique and ambitious undertaking should appear in the last quarter of the twentieth century—at a time when many people are redefining history to include accounts of those events closest to them, in other words, local history. Professional historians are now joining community people in their belief that history—real history—is rooted in local tradition.

In Tennessee, as in many other states, local history is synonymous with county history, for the county has always been the basic unit of governmental organization. Although Tennesseans have taken part in state and national government with interest and conspicuous success, it is at the county level that the majority of citizens have had the most direct contact with government.

Ninety-five counties eventually were established in Tennessee. Their boundaries sometimes followed natural divisions of the land; sometimes they were surveyed. Their size was generally determined by the distance a citizen could travel from the remote areas to the county seat and return in one day. Thus most counties were relatively small in size.

Although possessing many common state-wide characteristics, Tennesssee has within its borders enough variety for several states. From the nearly vertical forested mountainsides of East Tennessee, across valleys, plateaus, basins, and hills to the level alluvial plains of the Mississippi River Valley, the 95 counties, laid out across 42,244 square miles, reflect this diversity. Each is different from the others, and each has had its own colorful and interesting history.

Heretofore no reliable single collection represented the history of every county. The *Goodspeed* histories, often containing considerable historical inaccuracy when they were published, are now almost a century out of date. Consequently, both scholars and general readers have recognized the need for such a comprehensive approach to our state's history.

Tennesseans, perhaps because they have had such a dramatic and diverse past experience, have long sustained an unusual interest and pride in their state and community history. It is fitting, therefore, that Memphis State University Press has undertaken the Tennessee County History Series, for Tennesseans traditionally have been pioneers—people who have made history rather than those who have followed the leadership of others. Beginning with this volume, history—real history—will be made. In this respect, as in many others, Tennessee again will be unique. Tennessee—the Volunteer State—is proud to serve as pioneer and leader.

Joy Bailey Dunn, Editor
Charles W. Crawford, Associate Editor

To Gomer Davis Hoskins

whose research and work are reflected on every page that follows.

Mr. Hoskins did not believe in morbidly dwelling on the past, but he did believe there was truth and wisdom inscribed on one of the stone pillars in front of the National Archives Building:

> The heritage of the past is the seed that brings forth the harvest of the future. Study the past.

He believed we should not only cherish our state and national heritage, but our local heritage also. He believed that local history should be chronicled for those adults who wish to read it and that students should be encouraged in its study so they might better understand and appreciate the background of their county and town, and the development of present-day laws and governmental procedure under which they live.

These beliefs were very strong and vibrant during Mr. Hoskins' lifetime—so strong that their memory has inspired and directed those whose privilege it is to carry on his interrupted work.

Acknowledgments

No historical compilation would be possible without help from many people, organizations, and institutions. For assistance, information, advice and encouragement, deep thanks and appreciation are hereby expressed and acknowledged to those listed below:

Tennessee Historical Commission, East Tennessee Historical Society, and individual members of Anderson County Historical Commission as listed in the Preface.

Pollyanna Creekmore, Johnson City, Tennessee; H. V. Wells, Jr., *Clinton Courier-News;* Mrs. A. D. Crenshaw, Clinton; A. C. Duggins, Greenville; A. S. Jarnigan and Tom McCoy of Clinton; and the late Mrs. Sanford Weaver and Mrs. Mamie Adams of Clinton.

For Oak Ridge pictures, Office of Public Information, Oak Ridge Operations, U. S. Department of Energy.

For Norris and Norris Dam pictures, Tennessee Valley Authority, Knoxville.

For allowing county records research, the late former County Judge J. D. Yarnell, former County Judge Joe E. Magill, former County Administrator A. B. Slusher and County Executive David Bolling.

Research Departments of Clinton Public Library; Knoxville-Knox County Public Library; University of Tennessee Libraries; Tennessee State Library and Archives; Carnegie Library, Nashville; History & Political Science Library, Emory & Henry College, Emory, Virginia.

For special attention to copying old pictures and other photographic work, Gene and Louise Tipton, Clinton Art Studio.

For typing and other assistance, Dorothy J. Farr, Martha Frye, Susan Allen and Clyde B. Hoskins.

And to scores of others whose names are not listed due to lack of space or unintentional omission.

Preface

This volume is a brief, introductory history of Anderson County, Tennessee. It is a simple account of early, intermediate and contemporary life in the county, from arrows to atoms.

One hundred seventy-eight years of life in Anderson County lie between December 1801, when the county was created, and the present year, 1979. In the beginning the ground was literally strewn with arrowheads of Indian hunters who had roamed the land for a long time. Today some of that same ground is the site of part of the atomic city, Oak Ridge. Truly the weapons which Oak Ridge had a part in making would have been called "white man's magic" by the American Indian of 1801.

During these 178 years many people have moved into, and moved out of, the county boundaries. Some stayed, and they or their descendants are present-day residents. Regardless of whether they remained or moved on, they have each contributed something toward making the county what it is today. Anderson County has a precious heritage. It has tradition. And it is surely fulfilling a destiny not even dreamed of by its founders.

The primary object of this historical account of life in Anderson County is to set down in orderly fashion some significant local events, dates and names which need to be brought together and preserved for historical purposes. There is a distinct pattern to the lifestyle of Anderson Countians. Some local historians believe this to be a result of the unusual succession of four major and contrasting economic phases. These periods are so plainly separated chronologically that it is tempting to call them "the four ages of Anderson County." For purposes of identification at this point, they have been classified as:

1. A half century of agrarian life of the early settlers, which in some county areas bordered on the provincial.

2. The era beginning immediately after the Civil War and reconstruction days. These years saw the coming of the railroad, the development of the county's rich mineral and timber resources, and other important industrial progress. It was during this period that certain ethnic immigrant groups were attracted to the coal fields, bringing mining knowledge and skills. Their coming resulted in a blending of the charm of many Old World customs and cultures with those equally as fascinating, yet different, because they had emerged during the years of pioneer hardships of settling in a wilderness country.

3. The post-depression socioeconomic experiment of the 1930s, when the Tennessee Valley Authority was created by the federal government. TVA built in Anderson County the first dam of that great and complex system of dams which now exist in the Tennessee Valley. Then electricity was generated at Norris Dam and put into area rural homes which had never before used electricity. With the building of the dam came flood control. Clinch River, which became Norris Lake, furnished water sports and recreation. Reforestation and soil erosion control were started by a federally funded program. And the model town of Norris was built.

4. The atomic era, born of the exigency of winning a war. The "Manhattan Project" of World War II, which in the fall of 1943 began its secret work, culminated in an historical event which literally focused the eyes of the world upon Oak Ridge as the atomic city. Instead of vanishing as quickly and silently as it came into being (as some wartime projects have done) the city has become an integral and important part of Anderson County, with continuing peacetime nuclear research. Citizens of world renown

reside and work there, and many nationalities are represented in its population. This sophisticated, cosmopolitan city has its very foundation on several rich river bottom farms formerly owned by some of the pioneer settlers from the first of Anderson County's four ages.

The secondary purpose of this chronicle about life in Anderson County is perhaps not so worthy an undertaking as the primary aim, but proves to be an easier task to set down in words, and is a fascinating study. It is simply to follow each succeeding generation of Anderson Countians along their daily path of work, home life, recreation, and participation in religious, educational and civic affairs . . . to catch a glimpse here and there of progress made in the way of doing things and in the manner of living . . . to see a broadening of the collective viewpoint of the people . . . but above all, to portray "life in Anderson County" as it is and has been since 1801.

County history also repeats itself—over and over again. This pattern of repetition is easily followed, being woven into the everyday life of our ancestors and predecessors through each of the economic eras of the county. The pattern is there—whether life is primitive or sophisticated, meager or abundant, simple or elegant.

That every county should have a published history was the firm belief of the Anderson County Historical Commission, self-created and organized in 1955. Early members and interested persons included Mrs. A. D. Crenshaw, Dr. and Mrs. J. S. Hall, Mr. and Mrs. Gomer Hoskins, Mrs. Helen Kittrell, Judge and Mrs. Buford Lewallen, Mrs. Lamar Medley, Mr. Clayton Scruggs, Mr. T. L. Seeber, Mr. J. M. Underwood, Mr. H. V. Wells, Jr., and Mr. and Mrs. D. K. Young, all of Clinton; Mr. and Mrs. L. T. Williams of Andersonville; Mr. and Mrs. Eugene Joyce of Oak Ridge; Miss Mary Rothrock, Miss Emma Suddarth and Mr. R. C. Seeber of Knoxville.

All the members were interested, yet each had other responsibilities which conflicted at times. The organization was kept together and functioning largely by Dr. and Mrs. Hall, at least until some groundwork had been laid. Their home was headquarters and their hospitality warm and genuine. But an irretrievable setback occurred through the deaths of commission members D. K. Young in 1960, Gomer Hoskins in 1961, Clayton Scruggs in 1965, and Dr. Hall in 1967. Each had accumulated notes and papers of great value, some of which could be utilized by other interested persons. But most of the vast knowledge of local history that each had learned and remembered from extensive reading, research, and talking with older people was lost forever because it was not recorded.

In 1964 a state legislative act required each County Court to appoint a County Historian, who in Anderson County is the compiler of this volume. Eventually the threads were picked up and an effort made to use the materials on hand, supplemented by several years of research, in order that an authentic history of Anderson County could be completed.

*A*NDERSON County is situated in East Tennessee. It is bounded on the north by Campbell County, northeast by Union, southeast by Knox, southwest by Roane, and northwest by Morgan and Scott Counties. It is about 23 miles long and, from tip to tip at the widest point, about 26 miles wide. It is almost triangular in shape. At various times prior to its creation in 1801, the area now known as Anderson County was identified as a part of various geographic and political divisions, namely Knox and Grainger Counties of the State of Tennessee, Washington County of the State of North Carolina, the Territory of the United States Southwest of the River Ohio, the Cherokee Country, and so on. It was a part of the territory referred to as the "West" in the work of Theodore Roosevelt, titled *The Winning of the West.*

The county is much smaller now than when created, the present area extending over approximately 342 square miles. In the beginning the county was more than twice its present size, going all the way to the Kentucky line. In creating later counties in this section of East Tennessee, the largest portion to be taken off Anderson was removed by legislative action in 1806 and became a part of Campbell County. Later, in 1849 and 1850, Anderson County was again partitioned, with portions going into Scott and Union Counties.

A graphic description of East Tennessee's topography, of which Anderson County is a part, was printed in 1830 in a travel brochure put out by the East Tennessee, Virginia & Georgia Railway Company. It described the general course of the Appalachian system of mountains, which run in the same general direction in East Tennessee, enclosing the valleys of the Tennessee and Holston Rivers and their many tributaries, including Clinch River. Between the mountain ranges are innumerable ridges and hills, many attaining a great height, all running in the same general direction. Between these parallel ridges are beautiful and fertile valleys and streams of considerable magnitude. Walden's Ridge, a part of the Cumberland Range, traverses the county. Several spurs protrude from this ridge, which breaks the land considerably, although there is much good soil.

It was within these enclosed valleys in East Tennessee, inside the boundaries of Anderson and Roane Counties, that the United States government chose to establish one of its key atomic plants during World War II, the mountain walls furnishing the seclusion and protection necessary for such a project.

Clinton, the county seat of Anderson County, is located on the west bank of Clinch River, 170 miles directly east of the state capital of Nashville, and 559 miles southwest by west from Washington, D.C., the nation's capital. Clinton is eighteen miles northeast of Knoxville, and is situated about halfway between Norris Dam and Oak Ridge.

Natural Resources

Millions of years before the appearance of Anderson County, the forces of nature were at work here to throw up the mountains and control the flow of streams which have played an important part in the affairs of the county and are still doing so. These forces were responsible for creating the exact conditions necessary for the abundance of natural resources existing in Anderson County when the time came in the course of events for the area to be inhabited. Anderson County is well watered by natural streams, with Clinch River and its tributaries in the eastern section, and

New River in the west. There are numerous never-failing large and small streams.

The main natural resources of the county are considered to be streams and waterways, mineral deposits, forests, animal life, and soil. It would be impossible to list these in the order of their importance because, at different times in the county's history, each has played an important part in the county's growth and development. Chronologically speaking, we might say the streams and forests which attracted the Indians to the territory embracing Anderson County were also instrumental in causing many white settlers to decide "here is where we will build our home." Not only did the great forests provide logs for building their first houses and fences, but wild game abounding in the forests furnished food, hides, and furs. The small streams and springs contained sufficient water for drinking and other domestic purposes, while Clinch River was an important means of transportation. Fish from the streams constituted another valuable source of food.

There was good farmland to be cleared and cultivated by the early settlers, but aside from river-bottom land, much of it was found to be scattered in fairly small pockets, and the upland soil was thin. Thus, planters who were looking for large plantations of deep soil naturally gravitated to Middle and West Tennessee during the period of migration to Tennessee. Many prosperous farms have been developed and cultivated to advantage in Anderson County. But the majority of those have been, between 1930 and 1970, inundated by Norris Lake or absorbed as a part of the Oak Ridge area, or the Melton Hill Dam and Bull Run Steam Plant developments.

Coal far outranks Anderson County's other mineral deposits, although comparatively small deposits of iron, salt, lead, zinc, marble, onyx, limestone and sandstone have been found. In the early days of the county, the scant salt deposits were very important. It cannot be said that the mineral wealth of the county was responsible for attracting the first settlers, for discovery of their extent and consequent development had hardly begun at the outbreak of the Civil War.

The part each natural resource has played upon the stage of Anderson County life, in the years under consideration, will be reviewed as this study progresses into the industrial, commercial and social development of the county. Each principal resource has been prima donna for a while with a supporting cast of the first rank, as will be seen as each has its turn.

Our Heritage From The Indians

No Anderson Countian could reminisce very long about his county's background without a nostalgic recollection of "Indian lore" heard when a child, and the thrill he experienced when digging Indian arrowheads from the ground. The colorful, fascinating story of Indian life (including even the warfare between Indians and whites) is a heritage we will probably never discard— nor do we want to—because it is a heritage that is truly American. Considering this, any attempt to portray life in Anderson County would seem incomplete without some reference to Indian life and to the common bond (perhaps unrecognized at times) existing between the white man and the Redman—that of having lived on and loved the same land. This possessive love of our beautiful East Tennessee country could well be the Anderson Countian's first heritage from the Indians who preceded him here.

Immediately before arrival of the white settlers, the general area which embraces Anderson County was occupied and controlled by the Cherokee Nation. The Cherokee were possibly less warlike, and more colorful in their tribal ceremonies and customs, than were some of the tribes. But to insert here even the briefest possible history of this one tribe would consume too much space and become so involved that one could lose sight of the primary purpose of the study—Anderson County history beginning with 1801. It would also be a needless repetition of material in the many fine volumes of Indian life in this region written by eminent authorities.

It is generally conceded there were no Indian towns within the boundaries of the present Anderson County. However, the

Indian mounds which have been excavated in the county furnish evidence that a few scattered families probably did sojourn within the present boundaries. Reference is made here in the archaeological survey of Norris Basin which began in January 1934 and continued until July of the same year. The work was supervised by Major William S. Webb, Senior Archaeologist of the Tennessee Valley Authority, in cooperation with the Civil Works Administration, the Federal Emergency Relief Administration, and the University of Tennessee.

This survey revealed 23 sites showing definite evidence of prehistoric occupation in the Norris Basin area. Seven were in Anderson County. As listed by Major Webb in *Bulletin 118* (Smithsonian Institution, Bureau of American Ethnology), the Anderson County sites were Johnson Farm Cemetery, Taylor Farm Mound, Lea Village and Mounds, Cox Mound, Crawford Farm Mounds, Freels Farm Mound and Doan Cave. Their significance is explained in *Bulletin 118* and their exact locations described. The bulletin is available in public libraries. Other Indian mounds were found later in the county, the most recent being at the site of the Fish Hatchery in Clinton.

That the Indians held this area in high esteem is evident from the frequency of the word "Eagle" found in place names, such as "Eagle Bend," "Eagle Ford," and "Eagle Block House" in Anderson County, which we believe have come down to us from the Indians. "Eagle Bluff," now in Campbell but formerly in Anderson County, is another example. The Cherokee called the eagle their "great sacred bird" and considered it the chief of all the birds. The Eagle Dance is thought to be the most important of their ceremonial dances.

So, our second heritage from the Indians could be our own admiration for the eagle, which we sometimes call "monarch of the sky." Certainly this admiration carried over from the Indian to the white race, for in 1782 the U. S. Congress selected this great bird for our national emblem. And today, in an effort to keep the eagle from becoming extinct, it is afforded full protection by the federal government.

Pioneer Settlement

It is reasonable to assume that, generally speaking, only the most enterprising, hardy, courageous, and perhaps adventurous members of an already settled community in the colonies would strike out for wilderness territory to establish a new frontier and again face the privations and hardships that they knew from past experience would be inevitable. Only the barest necessities for the journey could be taken. On arrival they would start anew clearing land, building houses, fences, furniture and grist mills. They would take their food from the streams and forests. For long intervals they would be deprived of news from loved ones left behind. In many cases the Bible, used both for worship and education, was the only book brought with them. They knew all these things, yet were willing to push on once again to new country where unclaimed land was waiting, thus becoming the hardy, courageous pioneers of the land later to become Anderson County.

Settlement in upper East Tennessee had begun around 1769, and a little later the Watauga Association was formed. During this period Anderson County land lay waiting—almost unnoticed—while the Watauga settlers were becoming established and buying land from Richard Henderson's newly created land company. The land (still in the state of North Carolina) waited through the American Revolution, through the formation and dissolution of the State of Franklin, and during the first migration of settlers to the Cumberland River region and the founding of Fort Nashborough. Indian hostilities would decrease at times, only to flare up again as the Redman watched daily encroachments upon the land he loved; treaties were made and broken by both sides.

The land which was to become Anderson County was "back country," and no one except long-hunters like Daniel Boone and his companions or regularly organized scouting parties would venture into the area. Elisha Walden and his exploring party were known to have traveled the Clinch and Powell River Valley as early as 1761, Walden's Ridge having been named in his honor.

Earlier, around 1750, Dr. Thomas Walker was sent through this territory by the Loyal Land Company of Virginia. He was guided by a group of long-hunters and followed the bison trails across Clinch River and through the great mountain pass, which he named Cumberland in honor of the Duke of Cumberland. William Calk, one of the 30 settlers who accompanied Richard Henderson over the Wilderness Trail to Kentucky in 1773, wrote in his diary that on Saturday, April 1st of that year, the company crossed Clinch River and camped overnight on Cove Creek. So although this back country was known about to some extent, for a good many years after the settlement of upper East Tennessee it remained unsettled and for the most part untraveled.

It is believed that by 1790 some of the general area adjacent to present Anderson County was beginning to be dotted by settlers' cabins—little groups of them here and there, where a few families would decide to throw their lot together and become neighbors for the companionship, help, and protection they could afford each other. Knoxville was growing and had begun to look like a city. It was platted in 1792, Governor William Blount having established territorial headquarters there the year before.

The adventurous ones kept pushing on to the West and, at that stage of the westward movement, East and Middle Tennessee for a while comprised the western frontier. It was all a land of promise. Some of the migrators, however, did not get far from their first place of settlement, stopping whenever and wherever they found a place they liked. It is probable that Anderson County was largely settled in this manner; a few here and there who came into the area liked it and put down roots which became deep and strong. It has always seemed a land easy to love and adopt as one's own.

It is believed that the first house built in what was to become Anderson County five years later was the dwelling built by Thomas Frost in 1796. Coming from Lee County, Virginia, he entered a section of land about five miles south of Clinton (then Knox County) where he remained and raised his family. One of his sons was Elder Joshua Frost who was among the most powerful of the early Baptist preachers in the county. His ministry was of 50 years duration.

Tennessee was admitted to the Union June 1, 1796, and settlement of the state, including what was to become Anderson County, now proceeded rapidly. Many settlers came in with Revolutionary War grants, some of which were earned through military service and some of which were purchased. Summer was travel time, because roads were all but impassable during winter months. Everyone hurried to find land, build their cabins, and get settled before cold weather. Some, without land grants, came as homesteaders until they could acquire title to a parcel of land.

It is easy to visualize the almost steady procession of people on the road—some walking, some riding horseback, others in open farm wagons pulled by oxen perhaps, and still others in covered wagons. Families who had traveled by river looking for a place to settle occasionally arrived by boat or homemade raft.

Many nationalities were on the move, usually in groups or clans. Not wishing to be separated, they would try to acquire sufficient land where they could build cabins close together. An Anderson County example of this was the German colony led by Frederick Sadler, a wagon maker of York County, Pennsylvania, who, in about 1799 or 1800, settled in the area which came to be known as Dutch Valley. The colony consisted of Sadler and his seven sons-in-law with their families, named Bumgartner, Claxton, Clodfelter, Leinart, Lieb, Shinliver and Spessard. Descendants of some of these families are present-day residents of Anderson County.

Listed below are family names of some other settlers known to be living in the portions of Knox and Grainger Counties, which became part of Anderson County, or who moved into Anderson very shortly after its formation. Although the list was compiled from various sources, such as official county records of court meetings and building of the first roads, keepers of inns and ferries, jury lists, militia records and so on, it is not presumed to be a complete list of the first settlers.

Adair	Alley	Anderson	Asher
Adkins	Alred	Arnold	Ashlock
Aldridge	Alves	Armstrong	Austin

Avery	Denton	Hale	Kirby
	Dew	Hall	Kirkpatrick
Baker	Dobbs	Hanna	Kitchen
Benson	Dotson	Harden	
Bickerstaff	Duncan	Harmon	Lamar
Bird		Harness	Lamb
Bowling	Edwards	Hart	Lawler
Bowman	Elliott	Hatfield	Lay
Bray	England	Hawkins	Layne
Brazleton	Evans	Haynes	Lea
Brock		Hays	Leech
Brown	Farmer	Heard	Leinart
Brummett	Forrest	Hendrix	Lenville
Bullock	Foster	Hill	Lewis
Burrus	Friby	Hobbs	Lively
Burton	Frost	Hogg	Long
Butler	Fry	Hogshead	Love
Byrum		Holt	Luallen
	Galbraith	Horton	
Campbell	Gallaher	Hoskins	Mankins
Carden	Garner	Houston	Marshall
Carson	Gastin	Hudson	Martin
Chitwood	Gibbs	Hutson	Massengill
Clark	Gibson		May
Cloud	Gilbert	Inglish	MacAdoo
Cole	Goldston	Ingram	MacBride
Cook	Graham		McCoy
Cooper	Grant	Jackson	McCrackin
Crawford	Grayson	Jacobs	McDonald
Crozier	Green	Jeffrey	McKamey
Cunningham	Griffith	Jesse	McKinney
Curnutt	Grills	Johnson	McNutt
	Grimes	Jones	McPeters
Dagley	Guthry		McWhorter
Davidson		Keith	Medlin
Davis		Key	Menefee
Day	Hackworth	Kincaid	Meredith
Denham	Hagler		

Miller	Pratt	Sharp	Travis
Montgomery	Puckett	Shelton	Tunnel
Moore		Siler	
Morris	Queener	Simpson	Umstead
		Sinclair	Underwood
Nelson	Ragland	Slover	Ussery
Norman	Ragsdale	Smith	
Norris	Rains	Snodderly	Vowell
Nunnery	Reaves	Spessard	
	Reed	Standefer	Walker
Oliver	Rhea	Stanley	Wallace
Overton	Richards	Steele	White
Owens	Ridenour	Stevenson	Whiteside
	Robbins	Stinnett	Whitson
Parker	Roberts	Stone	Whitten
Parks	Robertson	Stonecipher	Willhite
Parsons	Ross	Stout	Williams
Patterson	Roysdon	Strader	Wilson
Patton	Russell		Wood
Pearson		Tate	Worrick
Peters	Sartin	Taylor	Worthington
Pollock	Saunders	Terry	
Porter	Scarbrough	Thomas	Young
Portwood	Scott	Thompson	
Potter	Scruggs	Tilman	
Prater	Seivers	Tipton	

Sixteen of these first settlers were, according to pension lists and other official records, veterans of the Revolutionary War. They were William Brummit, James Grant, Augustin Hackworth, David Hall, Thomas Elias Hoskins, Kinza Johnson, John Kitchen, Richard Luallen, John McAdoo, Joseph McPeters, Douglas Oliver, Thomas Parsons, Page Portwood, Henry Ridenour, Layton Smith, Obidiah Wood.

Other settlers moving into the county later who had also fought in the Revolution included James Alley, Isaac Armstrong, James Blackburn, John Bowman, Andrew Braden, Thomas Brummit, William Butler, Alden Byrum, John Chapman, William

Cross, Thomas Duncan, Joseph England, Micajah Frost, John Gasperson, Henry Goodman, William Graham, Joseph Hancock, William Hancock, William Henderson, John Herrell, Jesse Hoskins, Francis Hunter, Peter Johnson, Joseph Lannum, Rice Levi, John Liles, Ancil Manley, John McEntire, John McKamey, Abraham Mosier, Henry Nunnaly, William Patterson, William Parks, Martin Ridenour, Reuben Roberts, William Roberts, Joseph Rutherford, Bernard Slaughter, Aaron Smith, John Wallace, Richard Whelan, William White, Alexander Wiley, and John J. Williams.

Some Immigrant Influences on the County

Anderson County has been influenced by immigration in several ways. The changing aspects of its religious, political, economic, social and cultural life all bear witness to the fact that various ethnic groups coming into the county from time to time have left their imprint. Too, the county has been fortunate in this respect: Immigrants who found their way as far inland as East Tennessee within a reasonably short time after reaching the New World were, as a rule, an intelligent, strong, industrious type of people. In considering this, one theory noted that only those who were a little more frugal and aggressive usually had enough resources left with which to disperse themselves throughout the country after paying their passage to America. Many who were less able-bodied, or without funds, simply did not make the effort to go far from the port where they had disembarked. This was a major complaint of the port authorities during the years when thousands of immigrants were pouring into this country in a constant stream. This same lack of money with which to begin farming or go into business would have kept some in the seaboard towns where ready employment was available or where benevolent organizations had been established to assist temporarily those immigrants who were having a hard time. One striking result of the particular type immigrant making his way inland is worthy of note: With him moved the absence, or at least the lessening, of crime, disease and pauperism which plagued seaboard towns where large numbers came in faster than they could be cared for or sent to areas where work was available.

Of course there were important adjustments and concessions to be made sometimes, especially by the smaller immigrant groups; if there was no church of their faith, they worshipped with one of the majority groups. They knew America was a land where freedom of worship was encouraged, but it was also a democracy, and the minority had to submit to the majority many times and in many ways. However, devout religious faith was typical of many of the foreign born citizens who enriched Anderson County by choosing it as their home. Many examples could be cited of immigrants who organized small churches in order to worship in the denomination or faith of their choice. Others simply carried on services in the home. The latter practice was typified by the way this problem was solved by the French family of Phillipe Maire who came to Anderson County about 1890, bought property in Clinton, and remained to become outstanding citizens and craftsmen. They were of the Roman Catholic faith and, because there was no Catholic Church in the county, the large family faced an almost impossible transportation problem to attend church elsewhere. As a result, they graciously and inconspicuously carried on orthodox worship in the home. The parents were assisted periodically by a priest who came to Clinton by train from his parish in Knoxville. Another example a decade or so later was the Dave Wenders, a fine family of the Jewish faith. The only Jewish family in the county for a number of years, the parents saw that their children received religious education and training advocated by the Jewish faith in the home.

Each war which involved sending American boys to foreign battlefields or on tours of duty has resulted in some of the soldiers bringing home brides from various countries. Most of the foreign-born wives remained to become naturalized citizens, and each brought a bit of her own country with her. So it has been from the beginning, all through the years, that life in Anderson County has absorbed and reflected highlights from the personalities of all who have chosen to sojourn in the county, briefly or permanently.

Creation of the County

We who are prejudiced in favor of Anderson County say it is unique in many respects. This may be true to a certain extent. It is equally true, however, that the early history of a given number of counties in a prescribed geographical area, with parallel dates, would be much alike. Only in the names of people and places would we see much difference, but these are important differences when it comes to county history.

In a comparative study of East Tennessee counties of comparable size, we would find similar historical facts about such things as the legislative act creating the county; organization of the first county court; building of a courthouse, jail and stocks; laying out of public roads; fixing of tax rates and fees for inns and ferries; organization of militia; recording of livestock marks; indenturing of orphan children; care of paupers; and similar necessary work.

These things are all in the records of new counties as they are formed and begin to function as new political subdivisions. Thus, while we are fundamentally studying our own local history, we are at the same time caught up in a vastly wider study—that of seeing the whole American scene unfold before us, for our county history is but a minute part of the whole. It is a cross section of American life, yet people with the names and faces of our very own ancestors.

Then, as the infant county grows, there comes a time in its life (just as in the life of every person) when individual things begin to happen to that county which set it apart from its neighbors and make it different, if not unique. The county begins to take on identity and personality.

It is with these individual happenings in Anderson County that we are primarily concerned in this study. But as we progress toward these later happenings which give our county its own individual personality, we travel a route which leads through the excitement of many other new counties being set up in Tennessee and other states, and all the subsequent days and years when they are growing up and taking their places in a growing nation.

American independence was only 25 years old when Anderson County was born. Tennessee had been a state for just five years and was sparsely settled in the eastern portion. As the boundaries of new states were defined, counties were created within these boundaries, but with much larger county areas than today. In the beginning Tennessee had 11 counties. Because of bad roads and the distance involved, residents found it difficult to get to the county seat to pay taxes, attend court or general militia muster, or take care of other matters.

From time to time groups of people petitioned the Tennessee General Assembly to create new counties. It was because of two such petitions that Anderson County came into being. In September 1801 James Grant, who had served in the Revolutionary War and was a personal friend of George Washington, headed a petition bearing 113 signatures of Knox and Grainger County residents. It asked for relief from the long, hard trips which, if made in winter, were over roads almost impassable. Made in summer, these trips prevented residents from tending their crops for several days. Almost simultaneously with Grant's petition, 278 Knox County residents presented a similar petition to the Legislature. These petitions, which received favorable attention by the representatives, are on file and may be seen at the Tennessee State Library and Archives.

On November 6, 1801, a private act was passed and approved to take effect "from and after the 13th day of December next." The act was titled "An Act to reduce Knox County to its constitutional limits, and to form two new and distinct counties by taking part of Grainger County." The two new counties were named Anderson and Roane, and their birthdate was December 13, 1801.

The Legislative Act dated December 13, 1801, which simultaneously created Anderson and Roane Counties, fixed the boundary of Anderson County as follows:

> Section 2—That all that tract of county lying between the following described bounds, shall be, and is hereby made

and constituted a new and distinct county by the name of ANDERSON, viz: Beginning on the Chestnut Ridge where the Knox and Grainger line crosses it, thence north forty-five degrees west, to the northern boundary of this state, thence south forty-five degrees west, to a point from whence south forty-five degrees west will strike Walden's Ridge one-quarter of a mile above the gap of the Indian Fork of Poplar Creek, thence to the double springs of the east fork of said creek, thence a direct course to Clinch River, opposite the mouth of Hickory Creek, thence up the lines of Knox County to the beginning.

Two or three years before, James Grant had settled near the confluence of the Clinch and Powell Rivers in the area which was then a part of Knox County, later in Anderson County, and still later a part of Campbell County. He laid out the town of Grantsboro which is one of the oldest towns in Tennessee. James and his brother resided on a large farm and, while East Tennessee was not properly plantation country, the Grant farm and several others were called plantations.

After Anderson County was created, James Grant filed application for a Revolutionary War pension; it was approved. His file contained his original military discharge which was signed by General George Washington. Major Grant, as he was known, was quite an interesting character. After he came to East Tennessee from his former home in Connecticut, he helped organize Knox County's first Masonic Lodge, the Polk Lodge of Knoxville. Grant was Senior Warden and John Sevier was Master.

Grant was proud of the fact that he was a personal friend of Washington, and always carried with him some letters written him by Washington. Another memento of their friendship which he always carried, was a silver medallion made up of various Masonic emblems. It had been given him by Washington who, while President, was master of the lodge of which both he and Grant were members. This medallion is now in the Special Collections of the University of Tennessee Library in Knoxville. Major Grant was also said to have been a personal friend of William Blount.

Certainly Grant was one of the more colorful characters who played a part in early Anderson County history. A review of his close association with President Washington and other national historic personages is a vivid reminder of the American Revolution and its meaning to all Americans. Grant was the first chairman of the Anderson County Court after its organization, and he remained chairman until his farm was cut out of Anderson and made a part of Campbell County.

The County Is Named

Several historians have recorded the fact that Anderson County was named for Joseph Anderson, who was a member of the United States Senate at the time a name was selected for the county. Senator Anderson had been prominent for some years before this and, according to his biographers, was an exemplary man, held in high esteem throughout the southwest territory and the nation. It was presumably during his tenure as territorial judge and while living in Knoxville that he became so well known and respected by citizens in the area which was to become Anderson County as to merit their consideration a few years later when they were selecting a name for the new county.

Of German descent, Joseph Anderson was born in Philadelphia, Pennsylvania, November 3, 1757. He studied law, and soon after his graduation was appointed ensign in the New Jersey line of the Continental Army. He was at Valley Forge and Yorktown and, by the end of the Revolutionary War, had attained the rank of Brevet Major. He was admitted to the bar and practiced law in Delaware several years. In 1791 he was appointed by President Washington as one of three Judges of the Territory Southwest of the River Ohio, where he served until 1796. He was Trustee of both Blount and Washington Colleges about this time. He served in the U. S. Senate continuously from 1797 to 1815 when, upon retiring from the Senate, he was appointed Comptroller of the Treasury by President Madison.

Anderson was said to be a devout man, of sincere but unostentatious piety. He married a daughter of Alexander Outlaw,

JOSEPH ANDERSON. *Photograph courtesy U. S. Library of Congress.*

and among their descendants were Alexander Outlaw Anderson, a Senator from Tennessee; David D. Anderson and Miss C. G. Anderson of Knox County. After his retirement from government service in 1836, Anderson lived in Washington, D. C. until his death on April 17, 1837. He was buried in the Congressional Cemetery.

The County Seat—Twice Named

1801—Burrville

That the county seat of Anderson County was to be named Burrville was so stated in the Act creating the county. This was in honor of Aaron Burr, who was at the time Vice-President of the United States and a powerful figure in New York state and national politics. He had the previous year nearly been elected U. S. President.

Aaron Burr was a remarkable man. Many volumes have been written about him and much historical research done in the hope of uncovering new information about his life, actions, and sensational trial. He was perhaps best described by Walter F. McCaleb, author of *The Aaron Burr Conspiracy:*

> There is in American history but one Aaron Burr. He was at once man-of-the-world, student, madman, schemer, diplomat, leader.

And his devoted daughter, Theodosia Burr Alston, said:

> I had rather not live, than not to be the daughter of such a man.

After Burr's fatal wounding of Alexander Hamilton in a duel, and his involvement in the Western colonization scheme, the town of Burrville, by legislative act, changed its name.

1809—Clinton

> Be it enacted by the General Assembly of the State of Tennessee, that the name of the town of Burrville be and

the same is hereby altered to that of Clinton, and that the said town of Clinton aforesaid, be, and the same is subject to the same laws, rules and regulations, that the town of Burrville has been heretofore subject to, any law to the contrary notwithstanding.

So it was that on November 8, 1809, Burrville ceased to be, and Clinton was born.

At this particular time in United States history, the name Clinton was perhaps as prominent as any family name in the nation. Many towns and counties in various states were being named Clinton, honoring the Clinton family of New York state. According to historians Goodspeed and Foster, Clinton, Tennessee, was named for DeWitt Clinton, who was Mayor of New York City in 1809. Several years later he became Governor of New York state, and while in that office was largely responsible for planning and pushing the Erie Canal to completion.

Because of the fact that DeWitt Clinton was only coming into national political prominence at the time the town's name was changed, many local people have expressed the opinion that it might have been George Clinton the townspeople were honoring instead of his nephew DeWitt. In 1809 George Clinton had been nationally prominent for many years, having been elected U. S. Vice President in 1804 as a States Rights Democrat, and re-elected to a second term in 1808. (As a coincidence of possible significance, Aaron Burr was Vice President when the town was named for him.) Previously, George Clinton had been a member of the Continental Congress, Governor of New York, and in 1776 had been ordered by General George Washington to take the field as Brigadier General of Militia. However, there may have been some local connection or reason which would have made it logical for the town to honor DeWitt Clinton, as suggested by both Goodspeed and Foster. Both DeWitt and his Uncle George were highly esteemed throughout the nation.

The Legislative Act of December 13, 1801, which constituted Anderson County, contained several sections authorizing steps to be taken which were necessary to get the new county functioning for its constituents:

Section 3 appointed as commissioners Joseph Grayson, Kinza Johnson, William Lea, Solomon Massengale, Hugh Montgomery, William Robertson, and William Standefer. They were to fix a place as soon as possible, near Clinch River on the north side, between the Island Ford and where Samuel Worthington lived, for a courthouse, prison and stocks; to purchase land not to exceed 50 acres; and to lay off a town to be named Burrville with streets and alleys, reserving two acres near the center on which the courthouse, prison and stocks were to be erected.

Section 6 authorized the commissioners to advertise the town lots and sell them to the highest bidder.

Section 7 authorized the commissioners to build a courthouse, prison and stocks, paying for same with money obtained from the sale of the town lots.

Section 8 provided that should the sale of lots not furnish enough money for the erection of the public buildings, then the acting justices should, in term time, lay an additional tax not to exceed 12½¢ on each white poll, 25¢ on each black poll, 50¢ on each stud horse and 25¢ on each town lot, from year to year until the cost of building should be paid.

Sections 9 and 10 required the commissioners to make bond, payable to the governor, in the sum of $5,000, and that they lay before the court a just and fair settlement of all monies handled by them.

Section 11 set the time of meetings of the Court of Pleas and Quarter Sessions as the county court was then designated, to be held on the second Mondays of March, June, September and December, the first session to be held at the house where Joseph Denham then lived, with subsequent meetings at the same place until a courthouse was built. A small log courthouse was completed in 1803.

Until 1835 the justices were appointed by the State Legislature. The first court was composed of Justices James Grant, John Kirby, Solomon Massengale, William McKamey, Frederick Miller, Hugh Montgomery, Robert Pollock, Joseph Sinclair and William Underwood. Listed below are the first elected and appointed officials for Anderson County:

Sheriff	John Underwood
County Court Clerk	Stephen Heard
Register of Deeds	Kinza Johnson
Coroner	Joseph Grayson
County Solicitor	John Finley Jack
County Surveyor	W. S. Crawford
Entry Taker	Francis Vickery
Ranger	John McKamey

William Hays McClung was appointed Constable to wait on the court. Constables were appointed to serve with the various militia companies, there being no civil districts at that time.

It is noted here that the first court of the county, the Courts of Pleas and Quarter Sessions, was even more important than the later county court, because it took the place of all the several courts we have in the county today. It was county, probate, juvenile, trial justice, chancery, circuit, and criminal courts all in one. This was a carryover from the North Carolina system, and remained in such capacity until the Tennessee circuit court system was established in 1809, and the duties divided. The Court of Pleas was a judicial body composed of three justices and could empanel a jury. It heard civil and criminal cases, bound apprentices, probated wills, partitioned land, etc. The Court of Quarter Sessions met four times a year and was the legislative and chief executive body of the court, being a most powerful agent in county affairs. The political aspects were also quite different from today, one reason being that the county chairman was elected annually by the court members who had been appointed by the Legislature. One of the first items of business at the first session of the new court was the acknowledgment of a bill of sale for a slave, a Negro girl sold by Joseph Sinclair to Ebenezer Bryan.

The first will to be probated by the new court was that of Aaron Guest. The first road considered by the court to be built was one "from the Island Ford near the ford of Cole Creek to the lower line of Anderson County between Peter Avery's house and the foot of Walden's Ridge." The jury of view appointed to lay out the road consisted of John Armstrong, Isaac Brazleton, Henry Farmer, Henry Johnson, William Mankins, John McBride and Isaac Standefer. For many years the roads were laid out by a jury of view. After the road was approved, the court named an overseer and a person to select the hands to work the road.

The first license to operate an inn was granted to James Chitwood. The first jury was selected at the March 1802 term, the members being John McAdoo, Foreman; James Abbott, Nathaniel Davis, John Day, Nathan Hale, Jeremiah Jeffrey, Richard Linville, Page Portwood, Henry Russell, James Scarbrough, Joseph Sharp, Conright Willhite, and Samuel Worthington.

The Superior Court which would serve Anderson County when needed was also designated in the Legislative Act of December 13, 1801. *Section 12* provided that "Anderson County be annexed to the Hamilton District of the State of Tennessee, in the same manner, and for all purposes, civil, criminal and military, in as full and ample manner as any county in the state, and shall send three jurors to the superior court of said district." The first three jurors to serve in this capacity were appointed at the March 1802 term of county court. They were William Davidson, William Hogshead and James Scarbrough, to serve at the District Court held in Knoxville the fourth Monday of March 1802.

There were roughly six hundred families residing in Anderson County at this time, according to lists of taxable property and polls returned to the County Court in June 1802. These lists, compiled by Pollyanna Creekmore, were published in the *East Tennessee Historical Society's Publication No. 23,* 1951. They show the number of white polls, black polls, acres of land and their location, and the number of town lots.

The first public election in Anderson County for governor, members of the U. S. Congress and state legislature was held in 1803. It was on June 15, and there were three voting places: one at the county seat, one in the area of Robertsville, and one at Wallace's Cross Roads (now Andersonville). One inspector was present at each voting place: Arthur Crozier, James Butler and

William Underwood. The court minutes listed these three men as "suspectors of the election"—whether facetiously or erroneously is not known. Occasionally a bit of humor did appear in the early handwritten minutes when court proceedings were perhaps less formal and more leisurely than today. By law, all public elections were held under sole jurisdiction of the high sheriff of the county.

By state law passed in 1835, justices of the peace and constables began to be elected by public vote. A law of 1836 relative to election of the sheriff, trustee, register of deeds, circuit court clerk and county court clerk, provided that if two or more persons received the highest number of votes in equal number, the deciding vote should be cast by the election officer. The entry taker and surveyor were elected by the justices. Field officers of militia were chosen by vote of the respective companies, and these elections were sometimes held in conjunction with the election of county officials. It was in 1836 that the county was divided into civil districts. Each district was to elect two justices and one constable.

Early Economic Activities

Agriculture and stock raising, together with related trades such as blacksmithing, wagon and harness making, and maintaining grist mills almost entirely constituted the ways of earning a livelihood for the very early settlers. Although stock raising has never been a major occupation in this county, it was actually necessary for each pioneer family to raise some livestock in order to have meat, milk and butter for the table, leather for shoes, wool for clothing, horses and oxen for transportation and work animals; these necessities could not readily be procured in any other way.

There were few fences, and animals strayed. Proof of ownership was the owner's mark or brand, which was required to be registered officially by the county. During 1802, 27 brands were registered in Anderson County. If the animals wandered across the state boundary, or into Indian territory, there were serious problems. In 1804 the County Court authorized a pound built on the public square, to hold stray animals until claimed. It was the ranger's job to advertise and describe the strays in some gazette and to prosecute violators of the state's estray law. The office of ranger was considered one of the most important jobs in the county. Other early occupations included inspectors of cotton, ferrymen, and operators of sawmills, cotton gins, and carding machines.

At this point in Anderson County history, transportation and travel were difficult. In laying out the first county roads, the settlers followed the Indian trails and buffalo traces to a large extent, because it was apparent that both Indian and buffalo had an instinct which led them by the better routes from watering place to watering place, or from watering place to hunting and grazing lands.

The earliest immigrants coming into this immediate area usually came to Tennessee from or through Virginia or the Carolinas. Those coming from Virginia probably entered Anderson County down Big Valley Road into the northeast part of the county which we know as the Andersonville and Norris area. Coming from the Carolinas many crossed the mountains into upper East Tennessee and journeyed through Knox County into Anderson at Bull Run, or over the old Emery Road into the Robertsville area.

Clinch River has always been one of the main arteries of Anderson County life. Being a navigable waterway, stretching for miles and miles and joining with other navigable streams, it made long distance travel possible many years before the building of roads. There is no doubt but that from the beginning it has intrigued and beckoned aggressive and progressive men who knew the potential value of a waterway such as the Clinch. It has thus been instrumental in the continuous shaping of the county's future by reason of its existence and strategic location. The economic and recreational life of Anderson County has in a large measure been influenced by the river.

One of the earliest industries of which we have a record is that of the miller, whose grinding of corn and wheat was important to the householder. Those mills depended on water power to turn their wheels. While many were located on creeks and other small streams, it was desirable to be on or near the river. Because Clinch River was navigable, state legislation was necessary to insure its continued navigability. State legislators worked hard to aid industry, but with an eye on the value of the river as a navigable stream. The same thing applied to fish traps, by which some made a living. Both mill dams and fish traps were allowed to be built across a sluice of the river, so long as this did not obstruct navigation.

Boat building was another small early industry in the county. Some farmers brought their produce on flatboats down Clinch River to certain established places along the river bank; there they sold or bartered with other residents. *A History of Navigation on the Tennessee River System,* published by the Tennessee Valley Authority in 1937 states "the last stronghold of flatboating, so important in pioneer days, can be said to have been the Clinch and Powell rivers." For several decades the county seat of Clinton was the central market place for the county, although there were country stores at a few locations.

On very early maps of Tennessee, the river we know as the Clinch was called Pelisipi, believed to be the name the Indians gave the river. Information in Henry Gannett's *Origin of Certain Place Names in the United States* says the river was named "Clinch" for General Duncan L. Clinch, an early explorer.

Early Society

According to information handed down through the genera- tions, class consciousness among the early settlers in Anderson County was negligible. It might have been because the county was typical of this section of East Tennessee, where there were few plantations and a small percentage of yeoman farmers, which put the majority on somewhat of an equal basis. They all needed each other and were too busy making a home to worry about anything else. They helped one another at work and in sickness. At other times they got together to raise a cabin for a new settler, or shared responsibility to protect the settlement from dangers of the forest. It could almost be said that "nobody was looked up to and nobody was looked down upon, for any reasons except character."

Of the approximately 600 families residing in Anderson County in 1802, only 90 black polls were turned in. We do not know how many slaves the 90 black polls represented; however, only 55 families were reported as owning slaves, and 37 of these reported just one black poll. The majority of people in the mountainous section of East Tennessee did not believe in slavery. Many of the male slaves were said to be skilled brick masons and carpenters, and most female slaves excelled at fine needlework and cooking. Some early settlers were experienced in furniture making, carpentry, masonry, machine work, and glass blowing. Their spouses were adept at weaving, knitting, spinning, candle making, soap making, and other household skills.

Establishment of Basic Social Institutions

There were very few newspapers in East Tennessee in the early 1800s, and none in Anderson County. Tennessee's first newspaper, the *Knoxville Gazette,* began publication November 5, 1791, at Hawkins Courthouse (now Rogersville). It was moved to Knoxville in 1792, and was used by surrounding counties when it was necessary to publish legal notices in a newspaper. In many cases publication could be accomplished by simply posting a handwritten notice on the courthouse door.

In 1809 Tennessee was divided into five judicial circuits. Anderson County was placed in the Second Circuit, with Bledsoe, Blount, Cocke, Jefferson, Knox, Rhea, Roane, and Sevier counties. The Honorable James Trimble was the first judge of this circuit, and held a term of court in each county twice a year, the fourth Monday in February and August, hearing both civil and criminal cases. The judge and solicitor for each circuit were elected by the General Assembly. They usually traveled on horseback, staying in each county until the docket was cleared, usually three or four weeks. In 1812 the state was divided into six congressional districts. Anderson was in the third, with Bledsoe,

Campbell, Franklin, Overton, Marion, Morgan, Rhea, Roane, Warren, and White counties.

Sixteen attorneys were licensed to practice in the Anderson County Court during the period 1801-1810. It is thought most of them moved on during the early migrations. Only four of the sixteen names were found in later records of court and legal proceedings in the county. The four who apparently remained here were William Hogshead, John F. Jack, Thomas Paine, and Jacob Peck. After the courts were established, lawyers from nearly all the counties in the circuit followed the judge from county to county, building up a wide geographic area of practice. In each county seat there were usually one or two inns near the court-house where the attorneys would take lodging. In the evenings they would sit around the fire and again try the cases they had heard during the day. There were no organized bar associations in those days, but the story goes that quite a close fraternity of lawyers grew out of their circuit-riding association.

It would be impossible to accurately trace the progress of education during the first two or three decades of Anderson County. It was not until 1823 that Tennessee had a public school law and district commissioners were appointed; therefore a great deal of what we do know about very early education is from information handed down through families. Before public schools were established, some churches sponsored education for the children, with the preacher often the teacher. His salary was usually paid in farm produce instead of money.

Many of the pioneers and settlers of Tennessee country were cultured, notwithstanding an idea held by some that they were all unlearned. Of necessity, life was simple and rugged. But this does not mean that ignorance was tolerated by all. There are records of families who gathered around their hearthstone daily for Bible reading, prayer, and lessons, even though it was necessary to keep a loaded musket nearby as protection from the Indians and wild animals of the wilderness.

In 1806 a state-sponsored academy was established in each of several Tennessee counties. Anderson was one of those included. The legislative act gave the academy a name and appointed trustees. Union Academy was in Clinton, near the site of the present Clinton Elementary School. The first trustees were Hugh Barton, Arthur Crozier, Samuel Frost, Benjamin Parker, and Jesse Roysden. Although state-sponsored and partially state-funded, tuition was charged students. Later the trustees were appointed by County Court, to whom they accounted for funds received and disbursed.

Only one physician's name has been found in a study of Anderson County's earliest records. It was noted in a deed recorded in the Register's office describing a property location: "100 acres located in Wolf Valley on a small creek that runs into Clinch River at Dr. Palatiah Shelton's." Presumably he was a medical doctor. But in those days, difficult travel and distances between settlements made it impossible at times to reach a physician when urgently needed. Traditionally, the pioneer housewife learned how to prepare and administer simple remedies made from medicinal herbs and other materials. And a capable midwife was to be found in almost every settlement.

For sixteen years there was only one post office in Anderson County. The Burrville Post Office was established in 1802. Its name was changed to Clinton in 1809, when Clinton became the new county seat. Arthur Crozier was appointed first postmaster and served for 36 years.

Anderson Countians have always been known as a church-going people. Before meeting houses were built, services were said to have been held in homes, in frontier blockhouses, school houses, or outside under the trees, wherever a few people wished to gather. Probably because of its geographical location, Anderson County, for more than a century, was predominantly of two Protestant denominations—Baptist and Methodist.

The *Encyclopedia of Southern Baptists* states that "churches multiplied in the Tennessee Association along the banks of the Tennessee, Holston, and Clinch rivers, keeping pace with the advance of the frontier." On December 25, 1802, the Tennessee Association was organized by a conference of 19 churches meeting at Beaver Creek in Knox County. West Walker of Anderson County was one of the leaders in drawing up the Articles of Faith adopted that day. Three Anderson County churches were in the newly-organized association: the East Fork of Poplar Creek, Cole (Coal) Creek, and Buck Horn Valley. Hinds Creek joined in 1806.

In the realm of Methodism, Bishop Francis Asbury's *Journals* furnish vivid and thrilling accounts of the travels he and other preachers made over the mountains, fording rivers when necessary, in all kinds of weather, to organize Methodist churches and classes in East Tennessee. It is believed Asbury never came as far west as Anderson County, but missionaries and preachers who traveled with him did come into this area. One of these, mentioned in Asbury's *Journals* as a close friend, was the Reverend John Tunnell, brother of William Tunnell, who, in 1800, settled in what was to become Anderson County the following year.

The earliest Methodist Church in what is now Anderson County was probably Moore's Gap Church. Quoting from a school term paper of Margaret Rose King, we find that "located about seven miles east of Clinton, just off Brushy Valley Road, Moore's Gap Church has been somewhat of a community building from the time of its founding in the early 1800s. Serving as a schoolhouse until 1812, the church was also used to hold elections until 1853 when the voting districts were rezoned."

Quality of Life Led by County Inhabitants

Just as today, there were good times and bad times. If the old adage is true that "a busy life is a happy one" then the early inhabitants of Anderson County must have been reasonably happy most of the time. Their table was set with the simplest of foods, but from many accounts their diet was diversified and healthful. There was meat, both wild and domestic; vegetables from their own gardens, either fresh or home-preserved; wild berries and fruits; honey and sorghum molasses; homemade cornbread, biscuits, and yeast-risen lightbread.

Recreation and entertainment were of a local nature, sometimes, as with spelling bees, educational, and sometimes accomplishing needed work, as with quilting bees, corn shuckings, logrollings, or raising a cabin for a new settler, which would be followed by a feast prepared by the women, and then dancing far into the night. Every settlement had its musicians and square dance callers. Then there were the winter evenings when neighbors would gather around the fire at one of the cabins for a candy pulling, and to swap stories of their experiences since venturing into the wilderness.

There were many hardships to be borne along with the better things of pioneer life. At times the women and older children would have to work in the fields alongside the men. There were times of grave illness in a family when no physician was available. There was anxiety about family members and friends left behind because so much time was needed for mail to reach the settlements. There were encounters with hostile Indians and wild animals. Some slaves were mistreated, and some black families were separated by sale of parents or children to families in other locations so that they never saw each other again.

From available information it appears that the first buildings erected in Anderson County, exclusive of the typical frontier blockhouse, were of similar construction. The cabins were usually one-room log constructions, with either puncheon or dirt floors, large fireplaces for warmth and cooking, window openings without glass but with wood shutters which could be opened, and sometimes lofts where the children slept. The earliest churches and schools were generally one-room log constructions also, with fireplaces or chimneys used for stoves. Most early furniture was homemade from lumber cut on the owner's property, much of it put together with wooden pegs. Furnishings such as curtains, bedspreads, quilts, and table linens were hand-woven in the home.

The only known original structure in Anderson County of the type described above which still stands on its original site is the Yarnell house on Highway 25W, about three miles from Clinton, on the left side of the road going toward Knoxville. It was built in two sections. The original house was erected about 1800 by Jimmy Yarnell and is thought to have been used in the beginning as an inn on the stagecoach road. A later section was added to

The Yarnell house, built around 1800. Enlarged in 1863.

make the house larger, the date on the chimney being 1863, which would indicate the date the second section was constructed.

Impact of the War of 1812 on the County

Practically nothing has been found in recorded local history regarding the War of 1812. The United States Congress declared war against Great Britain on June 18, 1812, and several Tennessee historians have written that Independence Day that year was a boisterous occasion. They have also written that perhaps the general population did not react so much to the proposed expansion of U. S. territory as they did to their feelings that "Imperial Britain" had infringed on American rights on the high seas and were inciting the Northern and Southern Indians to wage war on the American frontier, which at that time included Tennessee. It is reasonable to assume that Anderson Countians shared the feelings of their fellow Tennesseeans and that a proportionate number of volunteers went from this county. It was during the War of 1812 that Tennessee became known as the "Volunteer State" because so many of her men volunteered for military duty.

Political, Economic, and Social Developments 1815-1860

Following the end of the 1812 war years, Anderson County experienced a slight economic upswing, despite the brief panic of 1819. The manufacturing census of 1820 listed the following small businesses and enterprises for that year:

12 Hat Shops	10 Coopers and Barrel Makers
3 Tanyards	3 Cabinet Makers
16 Blacksmiths	38 Sugar Manufacturers
5 Saddlers	44 Distilleries
5 Wheelwrights	

During the 1820s there were numerous land transactions,

mostly small tracts being bought by newcomers to the county. John Gibbs had purchased 5000 acres in sections "A" and "D" of the Henderson & Company survey from Nathaniel Hart, a member of the Henderson Company, and during the 1820s most of the 5000 acres were sold by Gibbs to residents in that county area. It was desirable farmland, and sold quickly.

Three hundred sixty-seven land grants were entered during the decade of the 1830s for Anderson County land. Scores of these grants were for 5000 acres each, located in sections of the county believed to be rich in mineral deposits. The total of these 5000-acre grants equalled more than the entire county acreage. This was because many of the large grants overlapped each other, while smaller claims had been filed for tracts within the larger ones. Lawsuit followed lawsuit, and while prior claims had precedence, it took the courts and attorneys years to settle some of the claims and define boundary lines of property owners. Some of these large grants formed the nucleus of the vast acreage acquired a little later by the landholding companies who leased land to the coal operators. Most of the large grants were dated in the mid-1830s and marked the beginning of the first definite steps toward developing the coal lands of Anderson County.

Large land grants and purchases in Anderson County continued during the 1840s and 1850s, many of them being speculation in "western mineral lands" by wealthy residents of New York, New Jersey, Pennsylvania, and Illinois. Some tracts changed hands without either seller or purchaser ever seeing the land.

Another brief financial panic was experienced in 1837. There were no banks in Anderson County, but some banking by local people was done in Knoxville, so the panic was felt to some extent. In those days individuals would take notes and loan money at interest. In 1837 one person was referred to during a business transaction as "the banking institution of Anderson County."

The year 1838 saw forced removal of the Cherokee Indians from Tennessee. There were still quite a few living in Anderson County. Some intermarriage had taken place before 1838. More

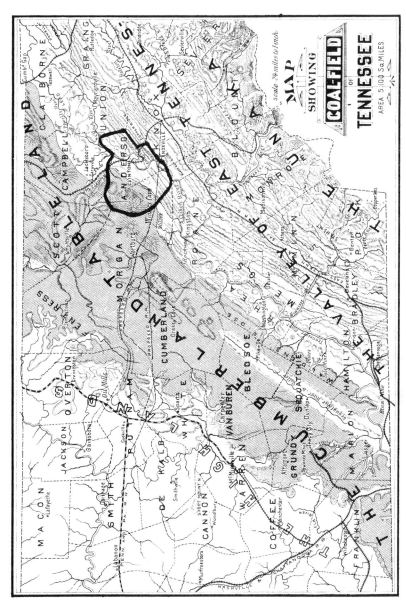

The "fluted" nature of the valley of East Tennessee may be clearly seen in this early map. The shaded portion shows that more than one-third of Anderson County

intermarriage was to take place later because many Indians escaped from the troops supervising their removal and fled back into the remote regions of the mountainous country they loved. Cherokee descendants in the county today are proud of their ancestry, and other Anderson Countians are proud of the contributions their contemporary Cherokee descendants have made toward the betterment of the county.

Partly as a result of the Jacksonian Democracy which had become popular in Tennessee, Anderson and other counties were affected by several state constitutional changes made in the 1830s and 1840s. Public officials began to be elected by popular vote; state legislators began to be apportioned and elected by the number of qualified voters in the counties rather than equal representation for each county; lotteries were prohibited; duelists were disqualified from holding office; and several other changes were made.

Railroad service in Tennessee began in 1851, but it was not until 1856 that rails began to be laid in Anderson County. The Knoxville and Kentucky Railroad Company began a line northward from Knoxville which would extend to the Kentucky boundary. Tracks were laid from Knoxville to the south bank of Clinch River, approximately where the railroad bridge in Clinton is now located, at the outbreak of the Civil War. All work on the road stopped when the war began.

In line with the state-wide attempts at internal improvements, in 1836 the General Assembly appointed four commissioners to study the possibility of improving the navigability of Clinch River. The commissioners were James Kirkpatrick, John Cross, and Samuel Moore of Anderson County, and John Ballard of Grainger County. A new stone, two-story county courthouse was built in Clinton during the 1830s, very close to the site of the first log courthouse.

Another internal improvement which had begun in the 1840s and 1850s and was being pursued diligently when stopped by the war was that of extending and improving pike roads in Anderson County. The war years changed many things, but the stoppage of road work perhaps retarded the county's economic development as much as any one thing, unless it was stoppage of the railroad, which so greatly affected the plans for large-scale coal mining.

Aside from the buying up of mineral lands previously mentioned, the mining of coal in Anderson County had been limited to individual operators. As early as 1830 James Kirkpatrick hauled coal by wagon from a mine above Coal Creek to Clinch River and boated it to Clinton. There were a few one-man and mule-operated mines about that time. Caswell Bowling made a coal entry on his tract of land above the old Baptist Church at Coal Creek. Quoting from *Goodspeed,* "Henry H. Wiley opened a mine on Poplar Creek, and for many years during the winter months boated coal down to Huntsville and Decatur, Alabama. He hauled the coal four miles to a point below the junction of the four forks of Poplar Creek, where it was put in boats, floated out that stream to the Clinch, then into the Tennessee, and thence to its destination. This mine was opened in 1852."

The Butler Iron Works was operating on Poplar Creek in the 1840s, as was the McKamey Forge near Donovan, and logging was beginning to be a factor in the county's industrial life. Hinds Creek was navigable for floating logs, and in 1858-59 Enoch Foster was bringing logs down the creek. He said, during testimony in a lawsuit, "It's easier to get logs down the creek than haul them to Clinton or Heiskell."

The Whig party gained state-wide momentum in Tennessee during the 1830s and was firmly established by 1840. According to the *Knoxville Journal & Tribune,* the Anderson County Whigs held a convention in February 1840, with Colonel C. Y. Oliver as chairman and J. Nickle as secretary.

Delegates elected to attend the Knoxville convention were J. M. Ashurst, John Black, A. Camden, Presly P. Chester, John Chiles, William Cross, James S. Davis, William Epps, John Garner, William Gibbs, James Hiatt, Martin Kennedy, Arthur Kirkpatrick, Thomas Lamar, John Leinart, David McAmis, Robert McKamey, Jr., Lewis Miller, Austin Moore, John Patterson, Robert Patterson, F. H. Robertson, James Ross, Lloyd Rutherford, Jonathan Scarbrough, Dr. Milton Tate, J. H. Tunnell, James Turner, John G. Whitson, and Samuel C. Young.

Regarding slavery, East Tennessee and Anderson County were in a peculiar position as compared to the rest of the state, and in even sharper contrast with the Deep South. Tennessee was slave-holding territory, but in Anderson County and some other counties in East Tennessee, there were comparatively few householders who owned, could afford, or needed slaves. There were several families in the county who had slaves as housekeepers or nurses for the children, and some planters or large farm owners who had a larger number of slaves to plant and harvest their crops. And there were a few merchants in Anderson County who bought and sold slaves for profit. At the outbreak of the Civil War, one Clinton merchant had recently invested $20,000 in slaves, who, he said, "left and were rendered worthless by the rebellion."

According to general information there were at least two public slave blocks within the county boundaries—one in the vicinity of Andersonville, and one in the Robertsville area. There was money made and money lost on slave traffic in Anderson County. From talking with older members of their families, a great many people agree that the quality of life of the slaves in Anderson County was perhaps a little better than it was in some places. This is not to say that there was no mistreatment of slaves, nor is it to say that there were no instances of slaves who ran away or otherwise misbehaved, because there are recorded instances of both. From time to time a few slaves were freed by their masters or mistresses before emancipation came about. Of course slavery was a state-wide political issue. Locally, from available records, it would appear that, while some county residents wanted freedom for the slaves and some did not, there was a very strong Union feeling on the part of many who felt secession was wrong.

During this period under consideration, 1815-1860, the Mexican War occurred. War was declared in 1846, and again Anderson County's young men rallied to the cause. William G. McAdoo, Sr., wrote a letter home soon after he arrived in Mexico in which he said most of his company were Anderson County boys, commanded by Captain John L. Kirkpatrick. He described walking to Knoxville where they took a steamer down the Holston and Tennessee Rivers to what was formerly called Ross Landing at Chattanooga, floated down the raging Tennessee, the Ohio, the Father of Waters, and across the Gulf of Mexico. Six of the boys died in service in Mexico: William England, Churchwell Hutchison, George W. Keeney, John L. Kirkpatrick, Jonathon Landrum, and William H. Leinart.

Other Anderson County boys who fought in Mexico included Charles Altum, Wiley Bailey, William Baxter, John Bennett, William Bennett, James H. Black, Roland Chiles, William H. Conner, Samuel Davis, H. M. Dobbins, Aaron Farmer, Felix Gilbert, Isaac Graham, Newton Graham, William Grimstead, William Hackney, Joseph Hardin, William S. Harrington, Daniel Henderson, W. R. Herrell, Warren Herrell, Lindley Hill, Michael Hostler, George P. Hoskins, John Jackson, Lewis Jones, John Keeney, Elijah Kerne, Henry Kesterson, William King, Jacob Levi, William Levi, James McDonald, Vincent Moore, James Morgan, Lee Nance, Joseph Romines, Armstead Wallace. Disability discharges went to Reuben Ashlock, James W. Hackney, Jacob Harness, Hamilton Hays, Elijah Jennings, George Jennings, Samuel D. Leinart, A. K. Oliver, and John Shaver.

Anderson County's first half century had seen the effects of several reforms. A new jail had been built in the 1830s, and care of the paupers had been carried on to some extent by the County Court since 1802. But the unfortunate children and adults who were mentally ill or retarded were in a class by themselves where not much had been done for them. There are early records where the County Court appropriated money to families who would be willing to care for a "foolish" or "crazy" child. After the poor asylum was established it became a refuge for the mentally afflicted or mildly insane adults who had no one to look after them. Apparently they were not closely confined, for stories have come down through the years about some of those mentally afflicted persons who day after day roamed the neighboring fields and roads, harming no person or thing, but within their minds living in a world which they alone knew. It was customary for families who had dangerously insane or uncontrollable members to keep them locked up and hidden. It was considered a disgrace to have such a person in the family.

In 1844 state schools were established for the blind and for the deaf and dumb. Court records show where Anderson County appropriated money to send children and adults to these schools in cases where the families could not afford the expense.

Union Academy was established in 1806 for male students only, but in 1817 the charter was amended to admit female students. This was a progressive move for Anderson County. It was not until 34 years later that it became mandatory under Tennessee law for all county academies entitled to a portion of the state academy funds to receive both male and female students. In 1847 a charter of incorporation was granted the Clinton Seminary Trustees, R. E. Cummings, William C. Griffith, John Jarnigan, John McAdoo, R. Miller, William Neil, and W. W. Walker. This was a Baptist school, located approximately where Fox Motor Company is now situated on South Main Street. In 1849 Clinton Grove Academy was chartered and built just across the street on or near the site of the present Garner-Sams Company. It was a Methodist school. The trustees were William C. Hutchison, J. M. Pyles, and F. R. Woodford.

The nation-wide separation of the Methodist Episcopal Church in 1845 into "Northern Methodists" and "Southern Methodists" is an interesting and revealing part of Methodism's history. It is especially significant in East Tennessee and Anderson County where there was intense feeling between family members and friends over secession and slavery. Many families were divided, some members for the Union, some against.

A humorous description of denominational prejudice in Anderson County is found in the book *From Sunrise to Sunset* by the Reverend Frank Richardson, a Methodist minister who came to Clinton Circuit in 1854:

> It was the bitterest denominational prejudice I have known anywhere. To make matters worse, political and denominational lines coincided for the most part. Most of the Methodists were Whigs, and most of the Baptists were Democrats. Dr. Tate was the Methodist and Whig leader,

and John Jarnigan was the Baptist and Democrat leader.
To show you how intense the prejudice was, at Clinton
they had Methodist and Baptist churches, schools, ta-
verns, stores, blacksmith shops, and ferries across the
river. Like the Jews and Samaritans, they had no dealings
with each other whatsoever. The rivalry became so great
at one time that both ferries were made free, and people
crossed the river without cost.

Any discussion about religious activity during the antebellum
period would be incomplete without mentioning the "old timey
camp meetings" associated with Methodism in the South. The
meetings were usually of one or two weeks duration, held annually in September when the crops were in. Gathering by the
hundreds, whole families came prepared to camp out the length
of the meeting. One such campground was located in Anderson
County near the present Sinking Springs Church. Each meeting
was a revival, with eloquent preaching by several ministers, and
singing of the old gospel hymns. Beginning in the early 1840s,
camp meetings were held annually at Sinking Springs campground for sixty or more years.

Politically, there was probably never so much confusion
before in Tennessee as there was just previous to and during
1860. Early that year several Tennessee groups—the Know
Nothing, American, Whig, and Opposition Friends—had a meeting and formed a "Grand National Union" Party, pledging
themselves to support the Constitution and the Union. All
groups—Republicans and Democrats, Conservatives and
Liberals—were confused and divided over a threatened split in
the Union and states' rights to keep slaves. The following figures
show just how strong Unionist sentiment was in East Tennessee
when the June 8, 1860 election was held. Total vote state-wide
was 104,913 for separation from the Union and representation in
the Confederacy, 47,238 against. Anderson County figures are
not available, but in East Tennessee, there were 14,780 for
separation, 32,923 against.

With the April 12, 1861 declaration of war, Anderson County

men began to choose sides and enlist. But after secession, things were different. Union sympathizers would quietly slip out at night and walk over Walden's Ridge and across Cumberland Mountain to Kentucky to enlist in the Union army. Every Tennessee county became a conscription center for the Confederacy, and all men of fighting age and ability who had not volunteered were conscripted for the Confederate army. "Eli's Cabin," situated part way up Cumberland Mountain, was the stopping place for the Union men. They were always fed, regardless of number, on fresh meat, cornbread, and coffee. They could not rest very long for fear of being overtaken by the Confederate scouts. They would then be piloted on across the mountain into Kentucky. By the time the pilot returned, another group would be waiting at the cabin.

There were no major battles in Anderson County. There was a rather brisk skirmish at Wallace's Cross Roads (now Andersonville), which is documented in the official records of the Civil War An eye witness who lived at Wallace's Cross Roads, J. K. P. Wallace, described the encounter in the *Anderson County News* of April 19, 1924:

> A battalion consisting of four East Tennessee companies of Confederate cavalry was stationed at Wallace's Cross Roads from early spring in 1863 until routed July 15th by a brigade consisting of about three regiments of U. S. soldiers who marched from Cumberland Gap, an important point 45 miles from the Confederate camp. The Confederates were very much surprised. They were almost completely surrounded, outpost guards were killed or captured, before the Confederates were aware of the pursuit by the federal forces. Evidently the Confederates had no sympathizers in the immediate country to notify them of the coming of the Federals. The Federals were piloted by the indomitable Captain "Stud" Reynolds who was familiar with the stretch of roads. The writer witnessed the flight of the Confederates from a point of vantage about ½ mile away. The scramble to get away, the

glistening of the guns, sabres and other accoutrements, made a thrilling spectacle. The Federals returned to Cumberland Gap as quietly as they came.

Stud Reynolds spoken of by Wallace was William Reynolds of Anderson County. He was originally a member of Company C, 11th Cavalry, but was detached and made a member of a scouting party, which became known as Stud Reynolds' Scouts. Reynolds made several daring and risky trips through the lines of the enemy.

Anderson County figured rather dramatically in helping to keep large convoys on the move carrying supplies for the Federal army, especially during the winter of 1863-64, by means of the ferry across Clinch River in Clinton. General Burnside, who had crossed on the ferry himself, made this statement: "The ferry in Clinton was an important one for the crossing of troops, trains, and animals, and its maintenance absolutely necessary for the good of the service."

In August 1864 a detachment of General Wheeler's command passed through Clinton and the Dutch Valley section of the county. A few years later some of the Anderson County boys in the detachment were brought to trial for their alleged part in what took place when the soldiers went through. Stories of "Wheeler's Raid" have been passed down through the years. Even today there are some who say the soldiers did it all. Others believe some of the residents committed part of the robberies, murder, and other crimes and blamed the soldiers for their own lawless acts. During the period 1866-69, actual court trials were held. The results of the trials are of record.

Several Anderson County soldiers were in Andersonville Prison. Some died there. James S. Scruggs, who survived prison life, told at length about conditions there. Judge W. R. Hicks, Sr. also told of conditions in Andersonville Prison. Judge D. K. Young, Sr., was stationed in Nashville in 1864 and told of helping with refugee work and raising funds to alleviate conditions. He spoke of seeing five men hanged who were bushwhackers.

While Anderson County suffered less than many places in

Tennessee, it was still desolate when the war was over, and efforts were made to resume normal life. Those who fought and those who stayed home had been undernourished during the war years. Many soldiers who made it home were sick, wounded, or maimed and never became able to earn a living. Farmlands had been pillaged and ravished; homes, barns, schoolhouses, and churches had been damaged, some burned; fences were down, and livestock had strayed. Many former slaves were at a loss to know how to become self-supporting; freedman's bureaus were set up to aid them; some simply stayed with the families they were with before the war; and many went north. With slavery gone, some of the larger land owners found it advantageous to cut their estates up into small tracts to lease or sell. The availability of these small tracts of land encouraged immigration. Tennessee was readmitted to the Union in 1866 and this brought a time of loyalty oaths before eligibility to vote, and in some instances confiscation of property in cases of proven disloyalty.

The blacks were given the right to vote on February 27, 1867, but were excluded from holding office or serving on juries. Soon the Ku Klux Klan was organized, one of its aims being to discourage the blacks from voting. There is very little recorded about activities in Anderson county by the Klan, the organization having been more active in Middle and West Tennessee than in the eastern section.

State-wide, politically,, the Republicans became a minority party during Reconstruction. The Democrats controlled West and Middle Tennessee and made some inroads into East Tennessee Unionism. However, the section of East Tennessee containing Anderson and several neighboring counties retained its Republican majority for about another fifty years.

Beginnings of the Industrial Era, 1870-1900

By 1870 commerce and industry were on the upswing in Anderson County. The development of the vast coal lands in this area and the building of railroads went hand-in-hand, each depending on the other. The coal operators had to have means of transportation for their product; the prospect of large coal shipments by rail assured the railroad promoters there would be sufficient revenue from that source alone to justify building a line through the coal region. This proved true in Anderson County, when, a decade or so later, for a period of time, the railroad company could not supply empty coal cars fast enough to carry coal mined in the Coal Creek and Briceville area. For several years Anderson County produced more coal than any other county in Tennessee.

In 1853 Coal Creek had one log house. In 1888 it had a population of 3000—more houses and a larger population than the county seat of Clinton. Coal Creek (now Lake City) is situated on the main line of the railroad serving the coal mines which had been opened during those years. The short-line railroads went through the town to the mines where the coal was loaded.

The first car of coal sent from Coal Creek by rail was in October 1867, by the Knoxville Iron Company, before the company was incorporated. On February 18, 1868, the Charter was registered with the State, the incorporators being Hiram S. Chamberlain, Joseph Richards, David Richards, and David Thomas, with offices in Knoxville. Previously the company had been operating a rolling mill in Knoxville, paying 16 to 18 cents a bushel for coal; then the stockholders decided to branch out and open mines of their own in order to get cheaper coal. They leased land at Coal Creek, started getting out their own coal, hauling it in wagons to Clinton, then shipping it on the cars to Knoxville until the K & K Railroad was extended to Coal Creek. After this, their shipments increased and in 1873 they were shipping about ten cars a day, each car containing ten tons of coal. They remained one of the larger coal operators in the county for more than fifty years. The various mines had identifying names, such as the Knoxville mine at Coal Creek which had 21 entries, and the Slatestone and Rose mines at Briceville. Some familiar names in the county of men who, over the years, were connected with the company in official or supervisory positions were John Chumbley, Floyd Peak, John Hightower, Charles Petree, and L. J. A. Petree.

The Black Diamond Coal Company began operating mines in Coal Creek about 1873, but was not incorporated under the laws of New Jersey until January 1882. Incorporators were E. C. Locke, W. J. Hornsby, T. H. Heald, W. B. H. Wiley, and E. F. Wiley. Their mines near the Coal Creek "Y" were named Black Diamond, Empire, and Shamrock mines. The Coal Creek Coal Company was organized in 1887 by E. C. Camp, S. P. Evans, Charles McKarsie, and E. M. Camp. E. C. Camp of Knoxville was company president. The secretary was D. B. Bean of Knoxville, and the superintendent was A. H. Bowling of Coal Creek. They had been mining and shipping coal since 1872; their mines were the Fraterville, Hollow Entry, and Thistle.

The Coal Creek Mining & Manufacturing Company is probably the largest land-holding company in East Tennessee, holding large tracts of land for leasing purposes in Anderson and some adjoining counties since 1872. The custom was to lease land to various coal-mining companies or to individuals by the year, for farming and stock herding, with liberty to dig coal for domestic use of tenants at such places as would not interfere with other tenants or agents. For use of the land, and payment of $1.00 per year rent, the tenant was to guard and protect the timber, using only such part as might be necessary for firewood and farming purposes, and to plant the fields in corn every other year. The company was incorporated February 14, 1872, in Roane County by W. S. McEwen, Henry H. Wiley, and Charles A. Bulkley. The main office has always been in Knoxville. Associated with the company for many years were B. Rule Stout and Forest Andrews of Knoxville. An office was maintained in Clinton for some years; there is now one in Oliver Springs. Detailed information about all the coal-mining and land-holding companies that have operated in the county cannot be given short of a large volume on that subject alone.

There were 21 commissaries or "company stores" doing business in the county during the 1880s and 1890s. Each operating coal company had its own commissary which was similar to a general store. They carried almost every item a family could need or want, including clothing, notions, house furnishings, hardware, staple and fresh food items. Some of the larger commissaries had an ice house where fresh meats were kept. They also had bakery items shipped in from a distance long before regular merchants carried these things.

For five or more decades the most commonly used means of exchange between miners and company stores was scrip. Scrip was a small metal token bearing the company name, similar to a streetcar or subway token. It was used by most coal companies as a means of extending credit to their employees. Too, in the early years, there was a scarcity of coins and currency due to there being no local bank. The company store was always conveniently located and the miners' patronage encouraged. They could draw scrip, which was borrowing against their wages, between pay days. Scrip could only be redeemed by the coal company who issued it, or by some individual who would buy it from the miner at a discount and later redeem it himself from the company. It became so easy to borrow heavily between pay days and the system became so widespread that it probably inspired the writing of the song "16 Tons" in which occurs the line: "I owe my soul to the company store."

Tennessee was the twenty-fifth state to create a Bureau of Mines, the first being Massachusetts in 1869. Tennessee's Bureau was established in 1891. The first Tennessee Commissioner of Labor and Inspector of Mines, George W. Ford of Knoxville, became well-acquainted with Anderson County during his second year in office, being called to Coal Creek often during the miners' insurrection. In 1892 he reported finding a few boys as young as nine years old working in some of the mines and gave orders not to allow any boy in the mines under twelve years of age. The boys were not supposed to be allowed underground, but were given such jobs as trappers guarding the doors. Ford reported one bad situation: "It is a sad sight, upon first entering the mine, to find a poor, weak little boy, only nine years old, compelled to stand in water and filth such as is found in the passageway, and remain there day after day and witness the passing by of this convict gang going to and from their daily work." Most Anderson County mines were reported to be above the average in safety to workers, ventilation, and drainage.

Many experienced miners came to Anderson County from Wales. There most had belonged to collier lodges and knew something about organized labor. In 1873 miners in the Coal Creek and Briceville area organized the Miners' Mechanics' and Laborers' Benevolent Association of Coal Creek, Tennessee. When it was chartered December 3, 1873, the "of Coal Creek, Tennessee" was changed to "of Tennessee." Many provisions in the Constitution and By-Laws of the Benevolent Association were similar to those of the United Mine Workers of America, established January 25, 1890. During the 1890s concentrated attempts were made by the UMWA to organize all miners of Coal Creek. This was partially accomplished, but all the miners were not organized until after the turn of the century.

Because the state treasury was on the verge of bankruptcy at the close of the Civil War and because of overcrowded and unhealthful conditions at the state penitentiary, the Tennessee General Assembly passed an act in 1865 "to lease out the penitentiary." Other Southern states were doing the same. Despite criticism from many sources, the system was in effect nearly three decades. The directors of the penitentiary leased the prisoners to various employers who became the "lessees." Several coal companies in Anderson County employed convict labor, especially in times of strikes. However, since it was much less expensive to use prisoners in the mines, the practice grew until hundreds of experienced miners with families to support were out of work. There were other undesirable facets, such as stockades being built close to the mining camps where state guards were employed to prevent escape of the prisoners; the alleged mistreatment of prisoners by guards; and other instances of abuse. Although some convicts had been used in Anderson County mines for 15 years, a climax was reached July 5, 1891, when serious differences between one of the coal operators and laborers remained unreconciled. The Tennessee Mine at Briceville brought in 40 convicts. They were immediately put to work tearing down dwelling houses of the former miners and building a stockade for the large number of convicts who would arrive shortly.

Absolute destitution and starvation were facing the free miners. All classes of citizens were angry. On July 15th the evicted miners took things into their own hands and, 300 strong, marched to the stockade at the Tennessee Mine and ordered the officers and guards to release the prisoners. Resistance was useless, and the miners escorted the convicts, officers, and guards to Coal Creek where the miners put the intruders on the train and sent them to Knoxville to await instructions from Governor Buchanan.

This was the spark which started the "Coal Creek War." The state militia was sent in and, for the first time in its history, established a permanent camp to keep peace and order. Following were three other revolts of the miners, during one of which several hundred convicts were turned loose in the mountains, speeded on their way with food, civilian clothing, and an admonition to "get lost." Some were never captured. There were several deaths. Court trials were held in an attempt to convict the rioters—an almost impossible undertaking because it was difficult to find witnesses who were not in sympathy with the miners. Finally a truce was reached in the fall of 1892, after the state officials showed willingness to abolish convict leasing at the end of the existing contracts. Burned stockades were rebuilt, and the convicts were returned with the militia where they remained until 1896 when the leases expired and the lease system was legally abolished.

Twenty-six leading American newspapers sent "war correspondents" to cover the insurrection, and several European newspapers carried day-to-day accounts of the "East Tennessee War." There is no doubt that what happened in Anderson County had a far-reaching effect in speeding up the abolishment of convict-leasing in other states. It was termed a form of slavery by several newspaper reporters who were on the scene. Several hundred miners came into Anderson County from Jellico and the Kentucky coal region to help the local miners. One incident involving the freeing of convicts took place at the Big Mountain Mine which is in Morgan County near Oliver Springs.

Lumber is another natural resource which has played a prominent and important part in Anderson County's industrial life. The height of the lumber business was in the 1890s and 1900s. Clinch River was used extensively to transport logs, and at high tide more than a hundred rafts could be seen at one time tied up at the Clinton wharf to be unloaded, while many others went on downstream to Chattanooga or other points of delivery. The loggers, strong and brawny men who dangerously rode the rafts down-river, would come into Clinton after unloading, looking for entertainment, a drink, and a place to spend their money. After a day or so in town, they would ride the crowded railroad coaches back to the timber country. Many of the logs unloaded at the Clinton wharf went to the Fisher-Burnett Lumber Company, which at that time employed 50 men. There were also the Gillis Lumber Company, Norcross Planing Mill, Simonds Planing Mill, Leinart Planing Mill, Knoxville Furniture Company, and a broom handle factory.

Clinch River pearls were an important source of income to many Anderson Countians before the waters of Norris Lake flooded the shallows where mussels were collected. Kunz and Stevenson in *The Book of the Pearl* wrote about the pearling excitement which had developed in the mountain regions of East Tennessee, especially Clinch River, around the turn of the century:

> These newly discovered resources proved so valuable that local interest became very great. Vivid and picturesque accounts were published in local papers reporting hundreds of persons as camping at various points along the streams, some in tents and some in rough shanties, others going from shoal to shoal in newly-built houseboats. They were described as easy-going, pleasure-loving people, the men, women and children working hard all day, subsisting largely on fish caught in the same stream, and dancing at night to the music of a banjo around the camp fires.

Clinton was the center of the pearling industry for this area. Saturday was trading day. Nationally known New York jewelers

STRADER HOTEL, 1906, J. C. Strader, Proprietor
This hotel was one of the principal pearl trading centers for out-of-town dealers. Those who have been identified are: (man left of lamp post with little boy) S. M. Hendrickson, Clinton pearl dealer, with son Allen, (man immediately behind lamp post) W. T. Strother, postmaster, (next man to right) W. E. Carden, farmer and business man, (next right, second left from post) W. W. Yarnell, farmer and large land owner, and (band member on extreme right) H. N. Guy.

were regular buyers of Clinch River pearls and made trips to Clinton to purchase them. Many times a single pearl brought a thousand dollars or more. Sam Hendrickson, Ross Hendrickson, and Vic Cagle were prominent pearl dealers in Anderson County. In 1900 rings and pins set with Tennessee pearls were featured at the Exposition in Paris, France. In the early 1900s Tennessee was one of the nation's six leading states in marketing fine pearls, and Clinton was listed as one of the three Tennessee towns known as centers of the pearling business.

The Zinc Smelting Works began operation in Clinton in 1881, and processed ore which was mined in Union County and brought down Clinch River in flatboats. An instance was noted in the local paper in March 1891 about a boat carrying 1300 sacks of zinc ore, weighing 15,000 pounds, that got away while being unloaded and went six miles downstream before being recovered. The plant ran day and night and made shipments to many U. S. and European markets. The company went out of business after about 20 years. Other industrial enterprises no longer in operation include the Clinton Stove & Iron Works, the Clinton Trunk Factory, and Hutton's Tanyards.

Reviewing the first century of Anderson County history, four towns emerge as having contributed significantly to the overall county economy. At the same time, through strong leadership, these towns have represented the strength and stability which was necessary for the county to endure wars, floods, major fires, financial panics, and internal insurrection. They laid the foundation for county participation in the tremendous advancement and achievements made possible by Norris Dam and Oak Ridge in Anderson County's second century.

Clinton

Clinton, as the county seat, has of course been the hub of county life; its industries having employed many people. A bank was organized September 20, 1894, which was the beginning of the present Union-Peoples Bank. Incorporators were J. A. Fowler, R. S. Kincaid, S. M. Leath, W. C. McKamey, W. L. Owen, E. A. Ross, Rufus Rutherford, C. J. Sawyer, and D. K. Young.

Clinton was where the Justices of the Peace gathered to make decisions affecting the entire county. It was where the city government, through its Board of Mayor and Aldermen, also made decisions and directed improvements and projects which not only benefitted Clinton residents, but reached out at times and helped citizens not residing within the town limits. Incorporated in 1890, the first Mayor of Clinton was D. R. Coward. The first aldermen were W. S. Cagle, Fletcher Clear, W. R. Dail, Sr., R. C. Dew, R. M. Dew, and Thomas E. Meehan. J. C. Scruggs was the first City Recorder.

During the period 1801-1900, law enforcement, town revenue and disbursements, education, health and sanitation, street building and maintenance, and street lighting were very important—just as they are today. The *Clinton Gazette* noted that one of the first matters taken up by the new Board of Mayor and Aldermen was improvement of the street lighting system. A sample gasoline street lamp was ordered for testing. A few months later twenty new street lamps were purchased; similar to their predecessors, the new style lamps burned gasoline instead of kerosene, thus making a much brighter light. The new lamps were to be installed on the principal downtown streets and the old ones moved to the outskirts of town. The *Gazette* said: "It was being considered by the aldermen that these older lamps would be placed near the residences of those who would attend to the lighting of them each evening."

Andersonville

Andersonville (formerly Wallace's Cross Roads) has from the beginning had a stabilizing influence on the economy and total life of the county. A few families had settled in the area before Anderson County was created and were influential in causing other desirable pioneers passing through to stop there and make their homes. One of the first settlers was John Gibbs, who entered a very large tract of land. Other early settlers included the family names of Carden, Clear, Hart, McAdoo, Ross, Rutherford, Sharp, Slover, Wallace, Weaver, and Whitson. A rural town, Andersonville was surrounded by many large fertile farms during the period under consideration. The town has always had good stores, mills, and other mercantile or commercial establishments.

The Andersonville Institute, a private academy sponsored by the Baptist Church, was established at Andersonville in 1897, and served many years as a "feeder" for Carson-Newman College. The academy proved to be one of the better church-sponsored mountain schools and attracted students from Anderson, Campbell, Knox, Roane, and Union counties. Many teachers in these and other counties were graduates of this educational institute. The first post office was established on February 23, 1849, with William Wallace as postmaster. Wallace served 38 years. It was Wallace's Cross Roads until November 7, 1888, when the name was changed to Andersonville. Henry Clear, Jr. had been postmaster three years when the name change occurred.

Coal Creek (now Lake City)

With the vast mineral deposits in and around the Coal Creek Valley, it had always been potentially important to the economic development of Anderson County. Because the surface land of that area was less desirable than other sections to the early settlers who were looking for farm land, Coal Creek and environs had only begun to be developed by the mid-1800s. Shortly after the Civil War, and especially after the railroad was extended to Coal Creek in the early 1870s, the coal boom started in earnest. It is difficult to discuss Coal Creek without mentioning Briceville, a mining town about five miles from Coal Creek, because some of the Briceville mines worked employees from Coal Creek, and some who lived in Briceville walked to Coal Creek to work in the mines there. It should be explained here that in the early days of opening mines in that area, Coal Creek village was farther up the creek toward the "Y" than the town is now. Too, Briceville and Coal Creek were rival towns to some extent, each trying to establish businesses and attractions to entice the miners' patronage. The year 1900 saw several mercantile establishments in Coal Creek, all doing a rushing business: restaurants, hotels, and an opera house for entertainment. The town had survived serious labor trouble, mine accidents, and the miners' insurrection, yet shortly after the turn of the century more coal was being shipped from Coal Creek than from any other county in the state.

The first Coal Creek post office was established March 6, 1856, with Joel Bowling as postmaster. Bowling had a large grist mill on the creek and coal land nearby where he made an entry and mined some in the 1850s. On August 23, 1888, the Anderson County Savings Bank was chartered and established in Coal Creek. Incorporators were T. H. Heald, Daniel Lee, James T. McTeer, M. S. McClellan, and Daniel Briscoe. Heald was president of the Coal Creek Mining Company and it is said that he organized and opened the bank for the benefit of the miners.

Oliver Springs (formerly Oliver's, before that Winter's Gap)

Oliver Springs is a tri-county town. It is located where three counties join and a portion of the town is in each county—Anderson, Roane, and Morgan. The first post office was Oliver's, established in 1826, with Richard Oliver as postmaster. It was discontinued in September 1866 and reopened in November of the same year as Oliver Springs with William C. Griffith as postmaster. The post office has been located in Roane County since 1897, but serves a large portion of Anderson County. The town has been largely a coal, lumber, and railroad center. In 1890 a bank was established in the Anderson County section of Oliver Springs.

Moses Winter was one of the first to enter land in that area. Professor Joseph Estabrook, President of the East Tennessee University from 1834 to 1850, retired to Anderson County. He was one of the first to discover salt in Anderson County. With the help of two slaves he operated a small salt mine near Oliver Springs for several years, although the deposit was relatively small and of a difficult nature to mine. E. A. Reed purchased land and was an early promoter of Oliver Springs. Joseph and Ann Richards and their family, John, William, Joseph, David, Ann, and Mary, came from Pennsylvania to Oliver Springs about 1880. They eventually owned coal mines, timberland, sawmills, and several farms. The mines were in Morgan County, but the

Mrs. Joseph (Ann Thomas) Richards

This lady typifies the many thousands of women who came from Europe and the British Isles to America when it was a young nation, and remained to make it their home. Ann Richards came from Swansea, Wales, to Pennsylvania in 1848 as the fiancee of Joseph Richards who came over earlier from Cardiff, Wales. She married, raised four sons and two daughters and worked alongside her husband until his death in 1888. Their descendants now live in many states. It was a grandson in Chapaqua, New York, a great grandson in Madisonville, Kentucky, and a granddaughter in Oliver Springs who contributed much information about the Richards family and the history of Oliver Springs, Tennessee, where the family lived for many years. Other Richards descendants formerly lived in Lake City, Tennessee.

Richards farms, homes, sawmills, and commissary were in Anderson County.

During part of the "gay nineties" period, the Richards family also owned a large summer resort hotel, or "watering place" as they were sometimes called, which attracted wealthy guests from this country and Europe. Situated on the Southern Railway, passenger trains regularly stopped at the hotel gate to accommodate guests leaving and arriving at the hotel. The hotel grounds covered eight acres and contained a picturesque springhouse enclosing several mineral springs, a grape arbor, croquet grounds, bowling alley, auditorium, ballroom, and park. Known as the Oliver Springs Hotel, it was located in Anderson County at the foot of Walden's Ridge, just outside the town. The hotel had 150 rooms, four stories, with a tower reaching 50 feet above the hotel for viewing the mountains.

County Politics 1880-1900

Attorney James A. Fowler, who later became Assistant to the U. S. Attorney General, was living in Anderson County at this time. He organized the Log Cabin Club in 1888, and was the Republican candidate for Governor in 1898. The Anderson County Republican Executive Committee members in 1888 were D. L. Hall, Chairman; J. A. Brown, Secretary; Elijah Adkins, S. L. Arthur, W. E. Baker, W. E. Brown, T. J. Campbell, J. M Carden, Oscar Chandler, J. B. Chapman, Reuben Craig, W. R. Dail, C. H. Duncan, W. R. Duncan, H. P. Farmer, Henry Forest, Levi Foster, D. H. Gibson, C. S. Hackworth, W. B. H. Hall, J. T. Hicks, G. H. Holt, G. W. Keith, C. R. Laughter, G. W. Leath, T. H. Leinart, W. H. McAdoo, Jerry McClellan, W. H. Maberry, H. M. Madden, Nicholas Massengill, Elijah Nott, John Overton, Dr. J. L. Price, J. L. Pyatt, A. T. Smith, Alexander Wallace, W. P. Weaver, and Elijah Woods.

The Democrat Executive Committee members in 1888 were R. C. Dew, Chairman; J. K. P. Wallace, Secretary; Sam Black, J. R. Cox, G. W. Foster, J. M. Foster, William Foster, John Hightower, Jasper Hoskins, J. C. Hoskins, P. M. Hoskins, W. W. Keebler,

T. S. Kincaid, J. M. McFerrin, William McKamey, William Miller, Sam Moore, Dr. W. N. Moore, J. Finley Patterson, F. P. Rutherford, Charles Shinliver, Dr. Henry Sienknecht, P. C. Wallace, and J. M. Yarnell.

Railroads Resume Activity

One day in October 1869 an extra holiday was declared in Clinton and all the stores and businesses closed. That was the day the first train crossed the Clinch River Bridge and passed through Clinton. At first there was one passenger train per day, but very soon long strings of freight cars went through daily, heaped with coal, signifying commerce with distant markets and work for local men. The next three decades were filled with railroad activity. The Knoxville & Ohio Railroad Company took over the K & K and began building branch lines to several mines. Private railroad companies were organized and building short lines. The Cincinnati Southern was showing interest in the area.

The second main line railroad to go through the county was the Walden's Ridge Railroad Company, incorporated in 1887 in Chattanooga. Coming from Oliver Springs, it went through Clinton, crossing Jacksboro Street (now North Main), connecting with the K & O at the Clinton Depot. On May 28, 1888, W. W. Keebler, the first contractor to break dirt on the road, drove a silver spike to celebrate completion of the road to Oliver Springs. Three days later the first car of coal from Oliver Springs by rail went to Knoxville, consigned to the Maryville Woolen Mills. By September 1888 traffic had increased so much that the tracks had to be laid with steel rails. There were six passenger and about thirty freight trains through Clinton daily. Before dining cars were added to passenger trains, regular stops were scheduled for mealtimes, and the trains would wait while the passengers got off and had a leisurely meal at a convenient inn. The Whitson House, the Southern Hotel, and the Brown House in Clinton were popular places for train passengers to dine, all being a few steps from the depot.

On March 3, 1898, the following ad appeared in the *Clinton*

Gazette: "WANTED—100 men to report to headquarters to make preparation to fight Spain." It had been hoped war could be averted, but on May 25 the Third Tennessee Regiment of Militia passed into the service of the United States. At the request of Colonel L. D. Tyson of the 6th Tennessee Regiment, Knoxville, X. Z. Hicks, A. E. Radert, and O. S. Scruggs of Clinton made up a company of volunteers to be known as the Anderson County Company. X. Z. Hicks was made Captain of the Anderson County Company and had received authorization from the United States Assistant Adjutant General to enroll a company for the 6th Volunteer Infantry. Captain Hicks left Clinton July 6, 1898, with 27 boys from Clinton, Coal Creek, and other parts of the county. The boys formed a line at the Clinton Inn, were given lunch, then boarded the train. They were taken to Camp Wilder in Knoxville where they camped a month before leaving for action. W. A. Brown wrote home in November 1898 stating the 6th U. S. Volunteer Regiment was stationed near San Juan. On January 17, 1900, Clem Jones, a member of the First Tennessee Regiment was said to be the one who captured the rebel flag at Manila. Seven years later Jones was appointed County Judge of Anderson County.

A new era seemed to have dawned for education in Tennessee with the passage in 1866 and revision in 1867 of the new school law. But it was several years before it turned out that way for Anderson County. Each county would now have a county superintendent of education. For Anderson County Charles D. McGuffey was appointed in October 1867. He reported to the State Superintendent of Education January 5, 1868, that because of an insufficient number of school houses Anderson County was unable to open schools in all the districts in time to draw the state school money. County officials and parents alike seemed to find it difficult to get started on the matter of education, and it was not until 1874 that any county tax was levied for schools. That year the Court levied 10¢ per $100 property tax for schools.

In 1875 the Tennessee General Assembly passed the "Charter Act" and during the years immediately following, Anderson and many other counties took advantage of state assistance in the building of private schools, academies and institutions. The land for the academies was deeded to the respective district trustees by the state. The following academies were built in Anderson County during the years 1877 through 1880: Big Valley Academy near Andersonville, Oak Grove Academy near Robertsville, Liberty School House at Scarbrough, Deep Springs School, Coal Creek Academy, Ross School House, Oliver Springs Academy, Zion Hill Academy, and Clear Creek Academy. By 1892 there were several privately owned and operated schools. At that time there were 58 public schools in the county, 21 log and 37 frame buildings. Five of these were for black children.

About half of the 5964 scholastic population was enrolled, with a little more than half of the enrollment in attendance. Only 25 pupils in the county finished the fifth grade that year in public schools. In 1886 the Clinton High School Company was formed. The Charter of Incorporation read, "The Business of said company shall be to teach any useful profession, trade, business, or art, and give instruction in any branch of learning, practical or theoretical." John Ross was president; the other officers were Henry Clear, H.C. Slover, S. L. Moore, and W. E. Brown. In 1889 the railroad tax was taken off, and the public schools began receiving more county money.

Here and there new Baptist and Methodist church buildings were appearing in the county, and during the 1880s at least one additional denomination gained a foothold. The large number of Welsh immigrants who came to the coal mining areas during that decade erected one Presbyterian Church in Coal Creek and one in Oliver Springs. Immigration had slowed considerably by 1900, although additional coal mines were being opened now and then which attracted new people to the area.

Despite accelerated efforts on the part of churches, temperance leaders, and prohibitionists, there were, during the 1890s, eight liquor dealers, eight licensed distilleries, five druggists licensed to sell liquors for medicinal purposes, and several saloons and tippling houses doing business in Anderson County.

The third courthouse to be built in Anderson County was erected in 1889-1890 with T. S. Kincaid and J. B. Carden respectively as county chairmen. It was built of brick along architectural lines popular at that time. It had a tower with clock, twin staircases in the front hall, and an unusual circular courtroom on the second floor. Each office had an individual fireplace and mantel, and the best steel vaults that could be bought. At the time it was built it was termed the second best courthouse in the state. The total cost was about $35,500. Twenty-five thousand dollars in bonds were issued by the court and were redeemed at the end of three years. The courthouse building committee members were Henry Clear, Jr., John Chumley, C. J. Sawyer, C. R. Low, and E. A. Reed, representing five distinct county areas.

The New Century, 1900-1917

On the morning of Monday, May 19, 1902, at 7:30, just after the workers had entered the Fraterville Mine, an explosion, said to be one of the most disastrous mine explosions ever to happen in America, occurred. Of the 184 men and boys who went in that morning, not one escaped death. Some were killed instantly, some escaped to small rooms or passages and lived a very short time, while others were able to get to some place in the mine farther away from where the explosion occurred and lived several hours, only to finally die from suffocation and after-damp. Unbearable heat and the effects of the after-damp prevented the escape of those not injured in the explosion. A few were able to write short letters or notes to family members, which were found in their pockets after the bodies were brought out.

The following quote is from an article appearing in the *Knoxville Journal and Tribune,* carrying an Indianapolis dateline of February 10, 1903:

> The national executive board of the UMW decided to inaugurate a plan of organization that will put men in every mining district of the United States in such force they hope it will be impossible for the operators to resist them long. Funds will be supplied to the organizers in whatever sum may be necessary to accomplish results favorable to the organization.

By May 22 all union miners were out in the Coal Creek valley. Notices were posted at all mines by District Number 19 officers of the UMW notifying the men to cease work until further orders. Operators who had contracts with UMW sent letters of protest to UMW President John Mitchell and to district officers Joe Vasey and John Bowden. A that time there were nine major mines in the Coal Creek valley. A mass meeting of 300 men was held and 200 men from the nine mines were detailed to visit the Tennessee Mine the next day and ask the non-union men to stop work. They blocked the Tennessee Mine entrance the following day and the *Knoxville Journal & Tribune* said: "If rumors circulated last night could be given any credence, there is danger of exciting times in the Coal Creek valley. The Union men seem determined to get rid of the non-union men."

All the mines were involved. There were strikes, alleged violence on both sides, houses were dynamited and damaged, threats made of whipping, along with conferences and talks which seemed to accomplish nothing. Briceville and Coal Creek suffered—families were frightened, business was bad. Negotiations and lawsuits continued until early in 1904 when Governor Frazier deemed it necessary to go to Coal Creek and speak to the miners who were on strike, appealing to their sense of fairness and public spirit. After the strike was settled, the UMW termed it to be one of the most successful strikes up to that time, gaining union recognition, a nine-hour day, and other job improvements. The strike, nation-wide, involved more than 100,000 workers.

In November 1905 a new business was started in Clinton. The name of the new company, manufacturers of men's knit socks, was Magnet Knitting Mills. The incorporators were Dr. S. B. Hall, S. M. Leath, C. N. Rutherford, Rufus Rutherford, C. J. Sawyer, W. W. Underwood, and W. S. Lewallen. Leath was president and Underwood secretary. A study revealed that women were particularly adaptive to textile work, but few women in this section had done factory work of any kind. The company wanted Anderson County women and men, and placed ads in the *Anderson County News*. Some of the first young women and men employed were

Lizzie Wallace, Bessie Dew, Nora Allred, Mossie Sharp, Edna and Minnie Norton, Gussie Wooten, Cassie Duncan, Ernest Young, Bob Brewer, and Joe Norton. The original work force numbered 30. Soon 30 more were needed, and so on, until peak employment in the 1950s reached more than a thousand.

Ladies' hosiery was added to the line in the early years of the company, which grew and prospered beyond expectations. Magnet became one of the largest hosiery mills in the South and one of the most progressive in the nation. Employees came and went, of course, but a large percentage were members of the 25-Year Club, many with 30, 35, or 40 years of service. There were a few who had worked with the same boss for more than 50 years. That "boss" was Carl S. Kincaid, who, as a very young man, was employed in 1908 as an office boy, but steadily advanced through various positions to become president for many years and board chairman. A. D. Crenshaw succeeded Kincaid as president.

On November 1, 1946, Magnet Mills, Incorporated began operating under an agreement with American Federation of Hosiery Workers, who had been certified as bargaining agent for the employees. Carl Wallace was the first president of Clinton Branch 125, AFHW, and Stella Duncan was secretary. In 1962 the plant was sold to Sam Burd and associates of Prestige, Incorporated, New York City, who continued operation until 1967 when the plant was closed. On April 21 Sam Ross, with 55 years of employment experience at Magnet, blew the mill whistle for the last time.

For 106 years a county chairman had presided at meetings of the Anderson County Justices of the Peace and performed other duties pertaining to the office. The chairman was elected, or re-elected, annually by the court members. This was changed by Private Act of the Tennessee General Assembly, effective September 1, 1907, which abolished the office of chairman of the county court. *Section 1* established the office of county judge of the County of Anderson. *Section 2* provided: "that the said county judge shall be a licensed attorney of Tennessee and otherwise legally qualified, and as soon as practicable after the passage of this Act the Governor shall fill said office by appointment, the

Carl S. Kincaid

A. Douglas Crenshaw

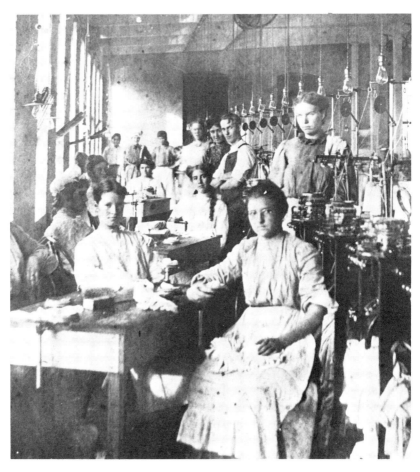

Hosiery workers in the early days of Magnet Knitting Mills

Clem J. Jones
County Judge 1907-08

James H. Wallace
County Judge 1908-24

Rufus Rutherford
County Judge 1924-26

W. A. "Alf" Brown   T. Lawrence Seeber
County Judge 1926-42   County Judge 1942-50

J. D. Yarnell
County Judge 1950-66

Joe E. Magill   Albert B. Slusher
County Judge 1966-74   County Administrator 1974-78

David Bolling
County Executive 1978-

person appointed to hold this office until the first general election for county officers occurring after the passage of this Act." An amendment in 1921 struck out the words "licensed attorney" and inserted in lieu of same "Person learned in the law." Governor Patterson appointed Clem J. Jones to serve as county judge until the September 1908 general election was held. James H. Wallace was elected. C. M. Harrington was county chairman in 1907 when the office was abolished.

In January of 1908 Clinton suffered an uncontrollable fire which destroyed 17 business houses and 14 residences almost within an hour's time. Following another disastrous fire that had taken place three years previously, the town had suffered quite a setback commercially and otherwise. Business firms in neighboring towns, individuals such as traveling salesmen who called on Clinton merchants, and various organizations contributed money, building materials, or labor to help rebuild the burned-out area. The Southern Railway Company offered a half rate on transportation for bricks and other materials to be used for rebuilding after the fire. By 1912 most of the rebuilding had been completed. Shortly after the fire the Clinton Board of Mayor and Aldermen adopted an ordinance which prohibited building wooden structures in the business section.

November 1, 1910, was the opening of the first new electric picture theater in the county. Located in Clinton, it offered shows three nights a week—Thursday, Friday, and Saturday. Admission was 10¢ for adults and 5¢ for children under 12.

A second coal mine disaster occurred in Anderson County in the early part of the new century. This explosion was on the morning of December 9, 1911, at 7:20, just after the men had entered Cross Mountain Mine No. 1 at Briceville. Eighty-nine men had entered the mine; 84 lost their lives, most of them dying from the effects of the deadly after-damp. A memorial service, honoring the miners who lost their lives in both explosions, was held on Saturday, December 9, 1912, at the Weldon Opera House in Coal Creek. Committees placed flowers on each grave. Twelve cemeteries were involved. Plans were made to perpetuate the memorial service each year, alternating the place for the service between Coal Creek and Briceville.

About this time a few automobiles and trucks began to appear on the streets and roads. The first motor car seen in the county made its appearance one day in May 1908. It was unloaded from the ferry near the hosiery mill and some workers spotted it from the shipping platform. Word spread through the mill in record time. Management allowed the employees to stop their work long enough to catch a glimpse of the car as it left the ferry and proceeded through Clinton on its way to Coal Creek. The name of the owner was not known.

It is thought that E. C. Cross was the owner of the first car in Clinton. R. A. Moser was the first automobile dealer, having a Ford agency located on Depot Street (now Market). Motor trucks began to replace the horse-drawn drays which delivered ice, hauled freight and express to and from the depot, and moved furniture. Motor vehicle registration became a law in 1915, and that year in Anderson County there were 15 automobiles, one truck, and two motorcycles registered. The first motor truck in the county available for hire or commercial use belonged to James M. Bailey. Other early truck owners were Henry Wilson and Eb Prosise. It was several years before the idea of motor freight transportation with larger trucks and long hauls was put into practice. Wiley Cassidy was perhaps the first owner of a franchised transport company in this county, for around 1930 he established the Clinton Transport Company.

Interurban passenger bus service was introduced into the county about 1918 by Avery Gamble and L. B. Williams. Williams, who probably had the first passenger bus franchise in Anderson County, was owner, operator, and driver between Coal Creek, Clinton, and Knoxville, accommodating many town and rural patrons. Williams sold his bus and franchise to Clarence and Alex Norman in 1921. They extended the run to Briceville and continued its operation until 1924 when interstate buses began service through the area after completion of the Dixie Highway. Other pioneer bus operators between Andersonville and Knoxville about 1918 included George Rutherford who later transferred his franchise to Condon Rutherford, Pete Rutherford, and Lester Lambdin. George also started a line between Andersonville and Maynardville. Luther Borum ran a bus service between Oliver Springs and Knoxville before interstate bus lines were established. Homer Goans of Minersville owned and drove one of the first taxicabs in the county. It was a Stanley Steamer, operated between Coal Creek and Briceville as early as 1914.

Motor vehicles were becoming more numerous every day and county roads had been improved considerably, but the big road news during the 1920s was that the proposed new Dixie Highway from Chicago to Miami was to become a reality and was to be routed through Anderson County. Financially it was a combined Federal-State-County project, and the County Court was to issue bonds in the amount of $53,000. The work of securing rights-of-way was begun in June 1924. This was one of the first north-south highways in the nation, and local citizens felt it was a boost to commerce and an inducement to industry to have it come through the center of the county.

As motor vehicles continued to increase in number and usage the County Court deemed it advisable to replace Clinch River ferries on the main arteries of travel through the county. In 1915 the court issued bonds in the amount of $75,000 for the purpose of building four much-needed bridges at or near the following ferries: in the town of Clinton near the hosiery mill, at Moore's Ferry on the Clinton-Andersonville Road, the ferry at Edgemoor, and the Massengill Ferry between Andersonville and Coal Creek.

Education was still having its ups and downs, but was making progress. In 1910 the water bucket and common dipper were still in use. The individual drinking cup was adopted in 1911 by the county board. By 1912 the county teachers had built up a Teachers' Library, which they decided to combine with the Clinton Library due to the difficulty in circulating their books. The Clinton High School was holding military drills daily for the boys, who were being taught the *Manual of Arms* by Dr. W. F. Broyles. The county's first Boys' Corn Clubs were organized in 1912. The clubs were sweeping the South with some 10,000 members. Good citizenship was stressed and the club provided a wholesome interest for boys of high school age. The compulsory school law was passed in 1913. Apparently many parents thought there was nothing to the law, one teacher said in a report, because "attendance improved very little until the law began to be enforced."

One of the major developments in Anderson County's history of education was undoubtedly the consolidation movement. Talk about it began as early as 1890, when the County Superintendent E. L. Foster said in his report to the state, "What we need is better school houses, and fewer. We need to effect a crusade against the little old dilapidated school house." In 1913 there were 67 schools in Anderson County. A. C. Duggins, who was elected county school superintendent in 1909 began just such a crusade as that advocated by Foster in 1890.

By 1915 consolidated schools in Anderson County were pretty well established, well in advance of most other Tennessee counties who were making an effort to consolidate. It was done in such a creditable manner that Anderson County was selected as a pattern and educators came from other states to study the system of consolidation here. Members of the county board of education at that time were William Mitchell, Dr. T. H. Phillips, W. J. Smith, O. R. Stansberry, and B. F. Wilson. Glen Alpine was the first consolidated school in the county. Transportation was effected by use of the new Tennessee School Wagon which had been adopted by the state. One of the wagons was placed on display in front of the courthouse, and was described by the *Anderson County News* as "a model conveyance and as comfortable as a railway coach in severe winter weather."

World War I

The United States entered World War I on April 28, 1917. June 9 was War Registration Day in Clinton and 174 men registered. A large crowd was in town for a patriotic rally and parade after registration. The county Exemption Board consisted of C. J. Sawyer, Dr. S. B. Hall, and J. C. Scruggs. By January 1918 people were being asked to observe meatless days, wheatless days, sugar-saving and coal-saving days. Anderson County had a large percentage of volunteers. Men were leaving daily from industrial, commercial, professional, and other phases of activity. Heavy wool socks for the U. S. Army were being manufactured at Magnet Knitting Mills and the company was advertising for women ages 16 to 45 to take the places of men who had gone to fight. Local people were doing their bit by purchasing war savings stamps and bonds.

As they left for the front, the soldiers traveled by train, and then overseas by boat, so there were long intervals when no letters were received back home or by the soldiers. In the meantime severe influenza epidemics were claiming lives of many people in the states. Christmas 1917 was very quiet, with special prayer services for the soldiers held in all the churches. Carl S. Kincaid was asked to head a local group in organizing a county chapter of the American Red Cross. When news came that an armistice had been reached November 11, 1918, there were prayer services of thanks held in churches, homes, places of business and elsewhere throughout the county.

Anderson County During the 1920s

Women voted in the United States in 1920 for the first time. According to local newspaper reports, Anderson County women seemed undecided about whether they wanted to vote, and very few turned out for their first chance at the polls. Apparently there was very little participation in Women's Rights movements in Anderson County. No record was found of public meetings or demonstrations.

Windrock Coal & Coke Company near Oliver Springs was expanding into one of the largest operators in the county, since opening Windrock Mine Number One in 1904. Owned by Bessemer Coal, Iron and Land Company, it was a large factor in the economy of Oliver Springs and surrounding area for nearly 60 years. The Windrock Company went out of business in 1961 and the old Windrock mines are now operated by Oliver Springs Mining Company. W. C. Hutchison and Elmer Sienknecht were general superintendent and office manager respectively for nearly the whole period of the company's operation in Anderson County. W. F. Haydon was general superintendent following Hutchison's retirement. Carl Keith, who became office manager when Sienknecht retired, is now with Lick Ridge Coal Company, with offices in Clinton.

Large coal mining operations were begun in the 1920s in the New River section of Anderson County, across Cumberland Mountain from the county seat. Charles M. Moore organized the Moore Coal Company in 1922 when the New River valley was an isolated area and the Moore family—Charles, Ed, Sam, and Bill— walked many times and sometimes went by horseback across the mountain from Petros. Fork Mountain Coal Company was formed in 1929, with B. E. Cheeley as President and T. J. Roberts, Secretary-Treasurer. Other coal companies on New River were the Diamond Coal Company at Buffalo and Rosedale, and the Thompson Coal Company at Stainville. The story of New River valley and its people is one of the most interesting phases of life in Anderson County—maybe one reason is that it is such an isolated part of the county isolated part of the county.

The two telephone systems—Old Cumberland Telephone Company and New Peoples Telephone Company—which had been in existence simultaneously for several years were beginning to be troublesome. The number of subscribers was steadily increasing, but the problem was that not everyone had the same phone system. They were designated the "old phone" and the "new phone." Only a few families had both. Those with only one phone were limited in the number of persons or businesses they could call. Consolidation was being considered by the two telephone companies.

The county agent and home demonstration work really came to the front in Tennessee and Anderson County in the early 1920s. But the real beginning in Anderson County was in 1912, even before the Extension Service became a legal educational arm of the U. S. Department of Agriculture on May 8, 1914, when the bill was signed by President Woodrow Wilson. It began here when the first boys' Corn Clubs and the girls' Tomato Clubs were organized in 1912. Mrs. Ella Johnson organized the first Tomato

Club with 4-H girls in Dutch Valley. Sue Dail (later Mrs. O. A. Lucas) was the first Tomato Club President in the county. A little later Mrs. Lizzie Longmire of Andersonville was elected president of a Home Demonstration Canning Club. The first County Agent for Anderson County, appointed on November 1, 1914, was A. S. Asmond. The value of the work of the organizations to the county is inestimable.

Prohibition during the 1920s in Anderson County was typical of other small Tennessee counties, with an average quota of "blind tigers" and private clubs doing business, and if certain telephone numbers were rung, a taxicab would deliver moonshine to doorsteps within minutes. Quite a number of moonshine stills were captured by the sheriff's office.

Amercian Legion Post 95 was organized June 25, 1920, with Randolph Shiflett as Commander. The post became inactive, but was reorganized in 1928 as Post 172 with Dr. O. D. Sanders as Commander. George Macres attended the Legion's organizational meeting in Paris, France, where he joined. He remained a member until his death in 1964. Bill Woods also joined while still in France during World War I. The American Legion Auxiliary was organized in Anderson County in 1932 with Mrs. E. W. (Eloise) Wynne as first president.

For a number of years before the decade of the 1920s several abortive attempts on the part of many people had been made to launch a broad program of waterways development in the United States that would include Muscle Shoals in Alabama and what was later to become the Tennessee Valley Project. As work progressed on the Muscle Shoals Dam between 1917 and 1925, it became increasingly evident that upstream storage projects were necessary. In the latter 1920s, after further study and reports by Army engineers and discussion in Congress, it began to look like the Tennessee Valley Project would become a reality. The Cove Creek site on Clinch River became more important. One could feel the mounting optimism and realization of what such a project would mean to the area.

The radio was introduced to many people during the 1920s. It was an innovation that not many families had when they first came on the market. One of the first radios in Clinton was owned by H.G. Amerine. He invited neighbors to listen to various news broadcasts and other programs, and soon radio parties were being given by others in the county as they acquired their wireless sets.

Bush Brothers Canning Company opened a plant in Clinton in July 1923. This benefited many families who had members employed there. Some years later the company purchased the McKamey farm near Marlow, a large farm, and grew its own vegetables for canning. This gave employment to additional persons.

City free mail delivery began in Clinton in March of 1926, and in April of that year the courthouse was wired for electric lights. The decade of the 1920s ended with the crash of 1929. One of the first layoff notices in this area occurred at the Southern Railway Company, which laid off 150 men that year.

The County During the Depression

James M. Underwood, Clinton attorney, was in college during most of the depression years. His father was also a Clinton attorney. Jim remembers that his father lost some money from stock he held in a Knoxville firm which collapsed during the Depression. Jim began law practice in 1936 and recalls he was not able to clear office overhead expenses during his first two years. He also remembers that one of the leading attorneys in Clinton at that time paid his experienced legal secretary $50.00 per month, perhaps the highest salary paid for any similar work during those years. According to Underwood, examples of some legal fees charged during the Depression were $2.00 for drawing a deed, $10.00 for a title, and $25.00 for an abstract.

Robert A. Moser, Jr. joined his father in an automobile dealership in Clinton in the 1930s, and continued the business after his father's death. Bob reminisces:

> Clinton and Anderson County were not affected as much by the Depression as most places. I do remember the

school teachers were paid by county warrants instead of regular checks. The warrants were cashed by banks or merchants at a discount. A good many cars were repossessed by the finance companies—mostly from men who had been laid off by the coal mines or railroads. The mines at Coal Creek, Beech Grove, and Briceville were kept running part-time by contracts they had with the railroad companies for coal. Bush Brothers Cannery coming to Clinton when it did helped the county a lot by giving employment to a good many people. Of course it was seasonal work—summer mostly because they canned beans, tomatoes, corn, peas, stuff like that. The cannery helped the farmers, too, by giving them quotas of certain vegetables to grow which Bush would buy to can. Some of the Clinton men—Sam Hendrickson, Al Carden, Claude Bush, and my father would "grub stake" the farmers by temporary financing. The hosiery mill never did close. It was put on short hours part of the time, but Carl Kincaid kept it running and stacked unfinished stockings to the ceiling to keep his employees from suffering. The two Clinton banks never did close.They merged because of regulations under President Roosevelt's banking law of 1933. They were both strong banks. All in all, this county didn't suffer nearly as much during the Depression as some places.

The Depression gloom was lightened immensely by news that a bill was signed by President Franklin D. Roosevelt on May 18, 1933, creating the Tennessee Valley Authority. One of the first acts of the TVA Board of Directors was to change the name of the Cove Creek Project to the Norris Project in honor of Senator George W. Norris of Nebraska who fought for over three years for the Cove Creek Dam in which he believed. Construction began October 1, 1933. The gates of the dam were closed on March 4, 1936, and storage of water began in the Norris Reservoir which covers 34,000 acres of land in Anderson, Campbell, Claiborne, Grainger, and Union Counties. The dam is located in Anderson

Group of several hundred workers at Norris Dam Campsite during lunch hour. November 6, 1933. *Tennessee Valley Authority Photograph H-115.*

County. The planned, beautiful city of Norris is also located in
Anderson County. Many books, articles, and treatises have been
written about Norris Dam and the Tennessee Valley Authority.
Most Anderson Countians (native or adopted) who have object-
ively read the history of the Tennessee Valley Authority in its
entirety became enthralled, for the county residents were too
close to the Norris Project's development in the county to
establish and maintain proper perspective. In the beginning it
was impossible to understand or even be aware of the fact that
they were in reality involved in a social experiment on the largest
scale ever attempted—one which President Roosevelt called "the
most interesting experiment ever undertaken in the history of the
world." The construction of Norris Dam, its impact on Anderson
County life, and the potentialities it created for the future constituted one of the major turning points which determined the
ultimate direction Anderson County's social, economic, and
political development would take. Anderson County and Clinton
native Lynn Seeber was general manager of TVA operations from
1970-78, after being in the legal division since 1952.

Beginning in 1934 Sunday school classes were begun in
Norris, and the first post office was established February 27,
1934, with George R. McDade as postmaster. This government-
owned construction town later became a self-governed munici-
pality—a model town. Also remarkable is that from that first
Sunday school class which was attended by all denominations
grew the idea of the Norris Religious Fellowship. The idea took
root and grew, nurtured by the desire of people with varied
religious backgrounds and from many parts of the country to
share experience and search together for spiritual enrichment—
not bound by creed or denomination. The first service was held
by the Reverend Charles C. Haun, a Congregationalist minister
and TVA worker whose religious involvement was voluntary.
Other denominational churches were built later.

World War II

With the probability of the United States becoming involved

Norris Religious Fellowship Chapel, corner East Norris and Dogwood Roads.

in war, selective service boards were appointed in all counties and National Registration Day set for October 16, 1940, when all men between the ages of 21 and 35 were to register. A total of 3,039 men registered in Anderson County. Selective Service Board members were A. D. Crenshaw, Dr. J. S. Hall, and E. W. Wynne. The Clinton National Guard was mobilized in February 1941 and left for training. On December 7, 1941, Pearl Harbor was attacked by the Japanese, and by December 11 America was at war. V-E Day was in May 1945 and V-J Day was August 14, 1945. Sandwiched between those various dates were more than forty months of fighting, injuries, death, and all of the other hardships and atrocities witnessed and endured by soldiers in the European and Far Eastern theaters of war. On the home front were the months of lesser hardships, the anxiety of waiting, plus the shock and grief when casualty news arrived. In the early days of war when American reverses occurred, there was acceptance at home that every phase of life in the United States would have to be directed toward winning the war against the totalitarian forces.

Of course the human side emerged now and then, identified by gripes of war ration books, blackouts, carpools, and other inconveniences. Anderson County made an excellent record of going over the top on the things that counted, such as purchasing U.S. Savings Bonds; participating in the selective service, war ration, and war production boards; replacing of men in industry and military duty by women; American Red Cross activities; and other phases of civilian participation in wartime. Tribute has been and will continue to be paid World War II casualties, heroes, and all men and women who were in the armed forces.

Part of Anderson County in Militarily Restricted Area

In July 1942 a group of scientists visited East Tennessee and gave their approval to the Wheat-Scarbrough-Robertsville-Elza section of Roane and Anderson Counties. A little later the U. S. Army decided that this would be the site of massive plants which were to be constructed. A federal Public Proclamation, dated March 25, 1943, announced that Courtney H. Hodges, Lt.

William C. Baker, Jr., Major General, U.S. Army

General Baker, a career Army man, was Chief of Staff of the 106th Infantry Division during World War II. He was a Colonel at the time. The 106th was the division who fought against such terrific odds to repel Field Marshall von Rundstedt's counter offensive toward Belgium in the Ardennes in December 1944, called "The Battle of the Bulge." One of the bloodiest battles of the war, the Ardennes fighting was described later: "The Lion Division took a tremendous toll of enemy shock troops, and wrote a story in blood and courage to rank with the Alamo, Chateau-Thierry, Pearl Harbor and Bataan." General Baker was a native of Anderson County and Clinton.
(U.S. Army photograph)

Commander Howard Laverne Lewallen

Commander Lewallen, who retired in 1969 with 27 years Naval service, took active part in World War II. He was awarded the Distinguished Flying Cross and Air Medal for participation in night operations against enemy shipping and shore installations. Commander Lewallen is a native of Anderson County and Clinton.

General, U. S. Army, Commanding Officer of the Southern
Defense Command, had designated Military Area No. 1 of the
State of Tennessee: a tract of land containing 56,200 acres and
situated within the Second Civil District of Roane County,
Tennessee, and the Eighth and Ninth Civil Districts of Anderson
County, Tennessee, it was known as the Clinton Engineer Works.
The tract was additionally designated and established as Total
Exclusion Area No. 1 of Tennessee. Thirty thousand acres, com-
prising several hundred individually owned tracts of land, were in
Anderson County. Court order and deed descriptions of these
tracts begin on page 513 of *Deed Book G-4* in the office of the
Anderson County Register of Deeds.

Anderson Countians were bewildered one morning to find
"war workers" sleeping on the courthouse lawn because no ac-
commodations could be found in Clinton. It was impossible to
cope with a situation which necessitated instant living quarters for
thousands of unexpected residents. Nevertheless local people
were proud to be a part of the war effort and soon opened their
homes and rented every available room to the newcomers.

Manhattan District . . . Clinton Engineer Works . . . Oak
Ridge—these are the names by which the project was designated. It was an undertaking of gigantic proportions, executed
swiftly. It was an important component of the part the United
States played in winning World War II. The 56,200 acres were
enclosed by an impregnable fence guarded by the army, with
four gates which admitted no person without a pass. Forty
thousand workers built the plants where 40,000 production
workers were to be employed. An average of one out of three
applicants was employed. There was a shortage of everything—
food, housing, and clothing. The stores had no gauge by which to
estimate demands. Prices soared. In approximately two years Oak
Ridge became the fifth largest city in the state, with 75,000
residents and many workers who were commuters. Roane-
Anderson Company built and rented or operated dormitories,
temporary housing, restaurants, cafeterias, hotels, permanent
housing, first aid stations, laundries, hospitals, dental clinics,
veterinary facilities, police and fire stations, area bus transporta-

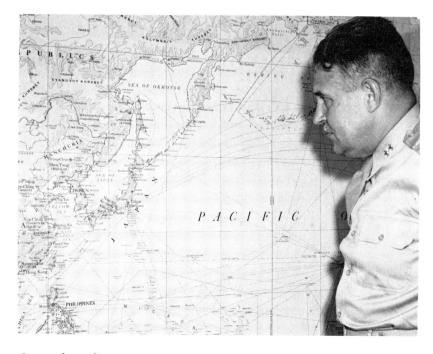

General Leslie R. Groves in Oak Ridge office looks at Japan.
Picture courtesy Office of Public Information, Oak Ridge Operations, U. S.
Dept. of Energy.

tion and terminals, truck farms, cattle and chicken ranches and many other things for the population of 75,000. Eastman Corporation, Monsanto Chemical, and American Carbide & Carbon were the contracting manufacturers. The first atomic chain reactor was placed into operation in 1944 by DuPont.

When information headquarters in Oak Ridge announced on August 6, 1945, that the radioactive heart of the atomic bomb began in the Oak Ridge facilities, the public was stunned. It was called the best-kept secret of World War II.

The United States Atomic Energy Commission (now Department of Energy) succeeded the War Department on January 1, 1947. The U. S. Army Engineering Corps left the area in 1949, and the gates of Oak Ridge were opened by Governor Gordon Browning on March 19, 1949, except for certain restricted plant areas which are still closed to the public. In 1956 homes and lots were offered for sale and the city was incorporated June 15, 1959. Now within the boundaries of the mountainous and formerly rural counties of Anderson and Roane was a city which belonged to all the world, dedicated to continuing research which can better serve humanity in peace times. "Atoms for Peace" became its slogan as Oak Ridge made its debut as an open city. General Leslie R. Groves, who was Commanding General of the Manhattan Project, had this to say about the historical significance of the city: "Oak Ridge will have a unique place in history. It will be a landmark in the field of atomic development." A. K. Bissell is mayor of Oak Ridge and has been most of the time since it became a city.

Post World War II Years

The density of population in Anderson County has shifted considerably since coal mining has declined. The Lake City, Briceville and New River sections, once thickly settled, have undergone a radical downward population trend. Lake City's loss is much less than the others because some new industries have come in; also, the town is situated on a highway where commuting to other towns to work is easier than from Briceville

Oak Ridge marks war's end. *Picture courtesy Office of Public Information, U. S. Dept. of Energy.*

Federal Office Building, Oak Ridge.
Houses Oak Ridge Operations, U. S. Department of Energy.

Picture courtesy Office of Public Information, Oak Ridge Operations, U. S. Dept. of Energy.

or New River. New River has suffered much more because of its isolation from the routes of travel and commerce. The new industries in the Eagle Bend Industrial Park and other places in or near Clinton have attracted many families. The farming and small village area formerly known as Edgemoor, Robertsville and Elza, which were sparsely settled before 1942, now contains a large portion of the city of Oak Ridge population which is over 30,000. The former rural area which is now the town of Norris has also changed the density picture. The following figures show a comparison between Tennessee's and Anderson County's population gains during the present century:

	Tennessee	*Anderson County*
1900	2,020,616	17,634
1970	3,024,164	60,300

Some of the industries which have come into Anderson County since World War II, excluding Oak Ridge, are Allied Structural Steel Company, American Forest Products Corporation, Anderson County Pulpwood, Inc., Armstrong Rubber Company, Brown Brothers Manufacturing Company, Fish Hatchery, FMC Corporation Bearing Division, Modine Manufacturing Company, Parkway Furniture Corporation, Sprague Electric Company, and Wel-Don Manufacturing Company. There is increased activity in the coal mining business, especially strip mining, in Devonia, Rosedale, Briceville and Windrock, and several coal companies have been organized recently.

One result of population increase and shift of density is that there is now less rural and more urban area in the county. When this happens there is certain to be social and cultural growth. With more and larger libraries, improved recreational facilities, the sponsoring of and participation in seminars, lectures, adult education classes, Playhouse, Little Theater, community chorus groups, ballet, opera, and symphony orchestras, challenge and climate are created which foster intellectual achievement and awareness.

This awareness has grown and flowered in Anderson County in many ways. A deeper regard for all people and their total needs is proven by the existence in the county now of the Regional Mental Health Center, Daniel Arthur Rehabilitation Center for children and adults, the People's Health Center at Briceville, Youth Haven, Hope, Rescue Squad, County Park, continuation of the County Fair, Community Services for Exceptional Citizens, Senior Citizens' social facilities, a continuing program of Little League Softball, Scouting, church-connected youth programs and many other activities which demand of their leaders volunteer commitment of self and time if they are to be successful.

Politically, beginning in the 1930s, the Democratic Party has steadily gained a large majority in Anderson County. In the November 1978 election a leading county businessman and Democrat, Jake Butcher, a Clinton resident, was the state-wide Democratic nominee for Governor of Tennessee.

The judicial structure of the county has undergone several changes in the last four decades. By Private Act of 1947, with amendments, a Trial Justice Court was established for Anderson County. *Section 2* enacted that "said Court is hereby vested with all the jurisdiction and shall exercise the authority conferred by the General Assembly of Tennessee upon the Justices of the Peace in the civil and criminal cases and actions, and the Justices of the Peace in all counties where this Act applies are hereby divested of such jurisdiction, power and authority." *Section 16* named J. Leon Elkins of Anderson County to serve until the first day of September 1948, and until his successor had been qualified and elected. A few years later the Trial Justice Court was combined with the Juvenile Court, the County Judge having heretofore handled juvenile matters. W. B. Lewallen was the first Trial Justice and Juvenile Court Judge.

Other judicial changes included instituting a new Law & Equity Court and making Anderson County the 28th Judicial Circuit. This eliminated Anderson's being included in a judicial circuit with several other counties which held court only three or four times a year. Roland Prince was the first Law & Equity (chancery) Judge, and Sidney Davis the Civil and Criminal Judge. The County Court (now the Board of County Commissioners) has initiated several progressive projects such as the County

Ambulance Service, Sanitary Landfill, Conservation Commission, Central Communications Center and Anderson County Utility Board.

Agricultural progress has kept pace with other facets of Anderson County life. Tractors and other motorized farm equipment have taken the place of many horses and mules. Many farms are now largely in pasture for dairy and beef cattle which formerly grew corn and other grain. Through advice of county agents and their own initiative, farmers are taking advantage of improved farming methods, better seeds, fertilizers and other advancements, and farm products are now being produced in larger quantity and better quality with less expenditure of money and man hours.

One of the Bicentennial projects in Tennessee was recognition by Tennessee Agriculture Commissioner Edward S. Porter of farms which had been cultivated by the same family 100 years or more. Anderson County reported five Century Farms under the Family Land Heritage Program. There have been direct descendants living on the Kinza and Sarah Johnson farm in Dutch Valley for 171 years. Present day residents on this farm are Mr. and Mrs. R. M. Farmer and Mr. and Mrs. W. C. Farmer. The William Riley Dail farm in Dutch Valley was established in 1855. Mrs. Floyd (Annie Dail) Hackworth and her three sons and their families still live on a portion of this farm; Fletcher Dail and his sister Lena inherited and have lived on another portion of the farm. The other three Century Farms are in the Norris-Andersonville area and are now owned by Mrs. Marie Wallace Hillon, Mr. and Mrs. Robert Irwin Longmire, and Mrs. Paul Longmire and Mrs. Rose Longmire.

One of the largest farms in Anderson County was the Young farm in Eagle Bend, which consisted of approximately 1,000 acres. A large acreage was purchased by the Tennessee Valley Authority, and other portions went for residential and industrial purposes. Mrs. D. K. Young, daughter-in-law of Judge D. K. Young, Sr., who developed the farm, was recently awarded with a plaque signifying that she is the longest continuing land owner in the county. The award was given by the Anderson County Board

The Young House

This gracious home was built about 1860 by Fairman H. Preston on a thousand acres of land in the Eagle Bend of Clinch River near Clinton. It was acquired by Judge D. K. Young, Sr., in 1865. Before being razed, it was for nearly a century the home of three generations of Youngs.

of Realtors. The beautiful plantation house on the Young property was included in the TVA purchase and has since been torn
down.

In the field of education integration was accomplished in
1956, following the 1954 Supreme Court mandate. There was
violence; the state National Guard was sent in to restore peace
and order; John Kasper, an outsider, was sent to organize the
white citizens' protest group; a minister was attacked and beaten;
on January 6, 1957, Edward R. Murrow presented "Clinton and
the Law" on his CBS-TV program *See It Now;* the Clinton High
School and some residences of black people were bombed and
FBI agents came in to investigate; Clinton students went to school
in Oak Ridge while CHS was rebuilt; KKK crosses were burned;
but Clinton High School had opened its doors to everyone and
integration was accomplished.

There was cooperation among school, town and county officials, and law enforcement officers. Frank R. Irwin was county
school superintendent; D. J. Brittain, Jr. was school principal;
and R. G. Crossno was school board chairman. W. E. Lewallen
was Clinton mayor; T. L. Seeber and J. D. Yarnell were county
judges during the time. H. V. Wells, Jr., editor of the *Clinton
Courier-News,* was nationally recognized for his reporting throughout the entire episode. There was increased emphasis on special
education during this period, and Mrs. Lucile Hill, Elementary
School Supervisor, worked very closely with the then new Daniel
Arthur Rehabilitation Center in Oak Ridge and its director Steve
Brody.

Following World War II, many new church buildings were
constructed on city streets and country roads. Instead of two,
three or four different denominations and faiths represented,
there were now 16. There was much enthusiasm in church work
during those post war decades.

Contemporary County Characteristics

Leisure Activities

Leisure activities are varied in Anderson County. Boating and fishing on Norris and Melton Hill Lakes are very popular during season, as is camping at the Anderson County Park and Norris State Park. For winter months indoor recreation facilities are excellent at the community centers in the county, with many programs and club meetings for adults and youth. Many men and women devote a great deal of their leisure time to civic and professional club work, which contribute immeasurably to many good causes, such as Civitan, Lions, Optimist, Business & Professional Women's Club, Bar and Medical Associations, to name a few.

Fine Arts Activities

Fine arts activities are numerous, with art exhibits, Little Theater and Playhouse performances, symphony orchestra and ballet programs, Timely Topics Club, and Ladies Wednesday Club. There are four outstanding museums in the county to visit: the Oak Ridge Energy Museum, the Lenoir Museum of Appalachian Artifacts near Norris Park, John Rice Irwin's Museum of Appalachia on Highway 61 near Norris, and the Children's Museum in Oak Ridge.

Leading Personalities of the County

Anderson County has produced numerous leading personalities, but space will only permit the mention of two—one contemporary and one of the earlier 1900s. Hubert F. Rutherford, deceased March 7, 1977, has been mentioned by scores of people as a leading citizen of the county over many years. He was with the Union-Peoples Bank for 52 years in several capacities from teller to president and chairman of the board. He was active in church and civic affairs and was very instrumental in getting new industry into the county. He made many trips with industrial board members and county officials to talk with prospective industrialists. Mrs. Rutherford was the former Melbe DeFord of Knoxville.

Judge Xenophon Z. Hicks, during his career, served both the county and state in judicial capacities. After practicing law for several years, he was Circuit Judge of the state of Tennessee and

Hubert F. Rutherford

Judge Xenophon Z. Hicks

went on to hold two Federal judgeships, sitting on the bench in Chattanooga and Cincinnati respectively. He was a Sunday School superintendent for more than twenty-five years, and every possible weekend he commuted to Clinton to be with his Sunday School pupils. No record has been found where a person who grew up in "Judge Hicks' Sunday School" ever had trouble with the law. His favorite hymn was "A Charge to Keep I Have," and whenever it was sung, his strong voice was heard leading out with the words he loved and in which he believed. Mrs. Hicks' maiden name was Effie Sawyer.

Local Literature

Folklore or Legend

A favorite legend of Anderson Countians concerned John Hendrix, who lived near the present site of Oak Ridge. He died in 1903. It was told that he assumed the role of a prophet around the turn of the century and prophesied the railroad's coming through that area; he also predicted that "Bear Creek Valley some day will be filled with great buildings and factories and they will help toward winning the greatest war there ever will be." This interesting story of John Hendrix and his visions while sleeping in the woods may be read in the first chapter of *The Oak Ridge Story* by George R. Robinson, Jr.

Some years ago J. K. P. Wallace of Andersonville wrote an article for the *Knoxville Sentinel* about the legend of a haunted stretch on the Indian Gap Road, once an Indian trail, and about an Indian Chief who died by the wayside and was buried there. It also told of a stock raiser who, while driving stock to the Carolinas on the road in later years, was murdered. Wallace told of later incidents about strange lights appearing and vanishing on the road, and about silent, ghostlike horses and riders accompanying travelers for a way, then disappearing, and other strange happenings.

Then there was an article by Pete Prince in the February 4, 1971, *Clinton Courier-News* about the witch of Dismal Creek who fought the Wolf Valley ghost; the articles also told of the witch's house on East Valley Road which has cast spells on its inhabitants for more than a hundred years. This is an area where the Indians did some killing and scalping before the pioneers settled there and where the notorious Harp Brothers had some trouble with the Indians. There are other folk stories and legends about Anderson County which are also fascinating.

Local Literature Figures' Work and Contemporary Literature

Some known local authors and their works are listed below:

Anderson, Margaret. *The Children of the South.* 1958. Farrar, Straus and Giroux, New York.

Braden, Beulah Brummett. *When Grandma was a Girl.* 1976.

Brewer, Alberta and Carson. *Valley So Wild.* A folk history. 1975. East Tennessee Historical Society.

Brewer, Carson. Columnist, *Knoxville News-Sentinel.* Current, weekdays and Sunday.

Fuis, Frank, Jr. *Too Wet to Plow,* with illustrations by the author. 1977. Exposition Press, Hicksville.

Irwin, John Rice. *Marcellus Moss Rice and his Big Valley Kinsmen.*

Jones, Guy M. *The Last Barnstormer.* 1971. Carlton Press, New York.

Joyce, Eugene L. *Private Acts of Anderson County, 1801-1956.* 1956.

Rogers, David. *Reflections in the Water,* a history of Lake City, Tennessee. 1976. A Bicentennial Project.

Seeber, R. Clifford. *A History of Anderson County, Tennessee.* 1928. Thesis, University of Tennessee, Knoxville.

_____. *Good Morning, Professor.* 1977.

Wells, Horace V., Jr. *A Story of City Government in Clinton, Tennessee.* 1951.

Young, Mrs. D. K. (Sally). *Through the Garden Gate,* a collection of articles reprinted from the *Clinton Courier-News.*

Newspapers and Periodicals—Current

Citizen-Times, Oliver Springs, weekly. Bob Woody, Editor. Serves tri-county area of Anderson, Morgan and Roane Counties. Oliver Springs *Citizen* and *Tri-County Times* consolidated August 4, 1978.

Clinton Courier-News, Clinton, weekly. Horace V. Wells, Jr., Editor and Publisher. *Clinton Courier* established August 1933. *Anderson County News* established December 1887. Combined June 1939.

The Oak Ridger, Oak Ridge, daily Monday through Friday. Tom Hill, Publisher. Richard D. Smyser, Editor. Established January 1949.

The Town Crier. Lake City, weekly. Larry K. Smith, Publisher. Joan Martin, News Editor. Founded 1956.

Norris Bulletin, Norris, weekly. Mimeographed. Mrs. Maurice Henle, Editor and Publisher. Established February 6, 1948.

Nuclear Division News, semi-monthly publication for employees of Nuclear Division—Union Carbide Corporation. James A. Young, Editor. Formerly *Y 12 Bulletin,* established August 5, 1944.

Summary

Without Anderson County and other counties like it, there would be no state—no nation. Putting them all together, we have America. Sometimes it has seemed that each county was predestined to play its own part in history. For instance, the exact resources and conditions needed were here in Anderson County—waiting—when a site was selected for the first of the eight tributary river dams and seven main river dams built by TVA during 1933 and 1944. Then, less than a decade later, U. S.

Army engineers found what they were looking for in Anderson and Roane Counties, a place to build war production plants during World War II. The topography was just right for seclusion and protection; TVA electricity was already here, together with the river and the railroad. So, the county gave of itself when the occasion demanded. Hundreds of families gave of themselves, also, when they abandoned their homes and moved, although they did not want to and did not even know why it was necessary.

Other times, during periods of grave trouble, Anderson Countians have proved to themselves, their state and nation that they could stand their ground for what they believed was right. From its beginning the county has sent capable and influential representatives to the Tennessee General Assembly to help make the laws of the state. Too, Anderson County has always furnished its quota of soldiers in times of war and has lost its share of soldiers on the battlefields. The county has grown, not only in population, but in stature also! Would that it were possible to name every individual and organization who had a part in making Anderson County history. It is not possible, but a few are listed below:

Sheriffs Of Anderson County

1801-12 John Underwood	1872-78 W. H. Gibbs
1812-32 Charles Y. Oliver	1878-84 J. A. Brown
1832-35 Richard Oliver	1884-86 T. J. Prosise
1835-36 Alexander Galbraith	1886-88 G. W. Moore
1836-42 Robert McKamey	1888-90 J. S. Kesterson
1842-44 Calvin Leach	1890-96 Rufus Rutherford
1844-50 Alfred Cross	1896-1900 A. L. Demarcus
1850-54 Calvin Leach	1900-04 G. W. Moore
1854-56 P. C. Wallace	1904-05 A. L. Demarcus
1856-60 John Rutherford	1905-10 D. F. Dagley
1860-62 P. C. Wallace	1910-1916 R. A. Smith
1862-66 George W. Leath	1916-18 L. C. Demarcus
1866-68 D. A. Carpenter	1918-24 R. O. Cox
1868-70 George W. Leath	1924-28 Charles C. Wade
1870-72 W. B. Robbins	1928-32 Cleve Daugherty

Sheriffs (cont'd.)
1932-34 W. R. Hicks
1934-40 R. A Smith
1940-44 C. H. Wells
1944-46 L. W. Bolton
1946-48 Joe Wilson,
         George West
1948-52 Bernard Vandergriff
1952-54 Joe Shoopman
1954-58 Joe Owen
1958-62 Glad Woodward
1962-68 Francis L. Moore
1968-74 Kenneth Caldwell
1974-76 H. H. Hill
1976-   Dennis Trotter

Trustees
1801-06 Thomas Hill
1806-16 Arthur Crozier
1816-36 William McKamey
1836-42 Aaron Slover
1842-44 Samuel Moore
1844-50 Barton McKamey
1850-52 J. H. Cox
1852-56 Levi Wallace
1856-60 William R. Dail
1860-62 John C. Chiles
1862-64 John Leinart
1864-66 David Dew
1866-67 John C. Chiles
1867-76 James A. Moore
1876-86 J. H. Hicks
1886-96 W. W. Hays
1896-1904 W. W.
              Underwood
1904-06 C. W. Cross
1906-18 George Taylor

Trustees (cont'd.)
1918-28 George Disney
1928-30 George Taylor
1930   Ernest Taylor
1930-34 George Rector
1934-38 Jerome Robbins
1938-46 Sue Braden
1946-52 Hugh M. Stokes
1952-56 Harlan LaRue
1956-74 George W. Ridenour
1974-   Patsy F. Stair

Clerk & Masters
1856-82 W. H. Whitson
1882-86 S. M. Leath
1886-1919 J. C. Scruggs
1919-20 W. B. Disney
1920-28 Sherman V. Brock
1928-36 S. T. Peters
1936-37 Ancil C. Bryant
1937-61 H. C. Scruggs
1961-   J. E. Lawson

County Court Clerks
1801-12 Stephen Heard
1812-34 Hugh Barton
1834-36 John Jarnigan
1836-44 William C. Cross
1844-52 John Key
1852-64 R. H. Coward
1864-68 W. W. Weaver
1868-70 R. N. Baker
1870-78 Robert C. Dew
1878-82 A. J. Queener
1882-86 Robert C. Dew
1886-1900 S. M. Leath
1900-14 W. B. Disney

County Court Clerks (cont'd.)
1914-26 W. A. Brown
1926-38 E. A. Hollingsworth
1938-50 Mattie
          Hollingsworth
1950-52 Lloyd C. Blackwood
1952-54 Mattie
          Hollingsworth
1954-57 Lloyd C. Blackwood
1957-58 T. R. Chadwick
1958-   John M. Purdy

Register of Deeds
1801-06 Kinza Johnson
1806-17 Arthur Crozier
1817-29 Daniel Leib
1829-32 William Dickson
1832-36 Thomas Hart
1836-44 John Garner
1844-54 John Overton
1854-58 R. M. Longmire
1858-61 B. W. Cross
1861-62 Samuel
          Worthington
1862-64 George W. Baker
1864-67 John L. Shipe
1867-68 William D. Keeney
1868-70 John Coward
1870-74 C. W. Cross
1874-78 J. A. Brown
1878-84 T. J. Prosise
1884-86 H. M.
          Hollingsworth
1886-90 T. J. Scruggs
1890-94 Joe B. Worthington
1894-1902 C. C. Reynolds
1902-14 W. A. Brown

Register of Deeds (cont'd.)
1914-20 George T. Riggs
1920-24 S. T. Peters
1924-46 J. T. Webb
1946-52 Ben Singleton
1952-56 Sam K. Carson
1956-   Joel M. Meredith

Circuit Court Clerks
1810-1836 Arthur Crozier
1836-44 John Jarnigan
1844-56 Milton Tate
1856-60 Alfred Cross
1860-66 I. C. Marshall
1866-68 E. W. Boren
1868-70 L. C. Cox
1870-78 W. D. Lamar
1878-82 D. L. Hall
1882-98 H. C. Slover
1898-1910 R. N. Baker
1910-18 W. C. Baker
1918-26 M. W. Taylor
1926-37 W. O. Duncan
1937-38 B. E. Ward
1938-41 T. J. Roysden
1941-42 Katherine B.
          Hoskins
1942-47 W. O. Duncan
1947-48 Eloise Wynne
1948-50 W. O. Duncan
1950-54 Duncan Copeland
1954-58 Phil C. Mason
1958-   Thomas J.
          Alderson

County School Superintendents
1869-72 Charles D.
          McGuffey

School Superintendents (cont'd.)
1872-73 J. C. Scruggs
1873-74 J. G. Hall
1874-76 R. N. Baker
1876-78 J. Allen Carden
1878-80 E. F. Taylor
1880-82 J. Allen Carden
1882-84 William M. Clark
1884-86 John P. Morton
1886-89 P. M. Hoskins
1889-92 E. L. Foster
1892-96 W. W. Underwood
1896-97 J. R. Evans
1897-99 J. N. Crowder
1899-1900 E. C. Cross
1900-02 W. B. Disney
1902-04 J. N. Crowder
1904-06 J. L. Barnes
1906-09 J. N. Crowder
1909-17 Allen Duggins
1917-22 W. H. Miller
1922-26 R. B. Wallace
1926-28 W. H. Miller
1928-30 R. B. Wallace
1931-36 R. C. Seeber
1937-48 Sherman Owen
1949-56 Frank Irwin
1957-62 James A. Newman
1963-68 John Rice Irwin
1969-   Paul Bostic

Present Board of
County Commissioners
H. Clyde Claiborne
Darrell E. Copeland
Jerry A. George
James M. Hackworth, Jr.
Charlotte Hayes
Robert L. Jolley
Jack Keeney
Q. V. Leinart
Helen Norman
Ernest Phillips
Jack Rains
Everett Sharp
Kenneth (Reece) Wallace

Anderson County Population

1810	3,959
1820	4,668
1840	5,658
1860	7,068
1880	10,820
1900	17,634
1920	18,298
1940	26,504
1960	60,032
1970	60,300

Anderson Countians who have served as Circuit Judges include Sidney Davis, W. R. Hicks, X. Z. Hicks, James B. Scott, and D. K. Young, Sr.; as Chancellor, J. H. Wallace, Roland Prince; as District Attorney General, David H. Cummins, William G. McAdoo, Sr., James M. Ramsey, James B. Scott, and D. K.

Young, Sr.; as Trial Justice & Juvenile Judge, J. Leon Elkins, Jennings B. Meredith, W. B. Lewallen, and Howard Woodside.

Anderson County Courthouse (1890-1965)

Anderson County Courthouse, dedicated May 27, 1967.

The Hemlocks

Formerly known as the Edwards House, now the Fowler House, it was acquired by Mr. and Mrs. Sam P. Fowler around 1900. Mr. and Mrs. Sam P. Fowler, Jr., now reside in the house and have restored it both inside and outside. It was constructed around 1830 by slave labor, with bricks made on the farm. Mrs. Fowler, Sr., is shown in the picture with children Alma, Lyman, Ruth and Sam, Jr. It is now on National Register of Historic Places.

Mrs. J. F. Dykes of Clinton (right) and guest, Mrs. R. S. Morris, of
Asheville, N.C., at the Appalachian Conservation Exposition held
in Knoxville in 1910.

First Macedonia Church, built in 1844. Rev. Luther Clear in doorway.

The Asbury United Methodist Church, Clinton, before it was destroyed by fire in 1947, with some of its members and friends.

Around 1920 when there were forty trains through Clinton, it took a lot of switching to side tracks in order to manage passage of the trains. Clinton was a railroad junction as well as water and refueling station. This switch engine saw a lot of service with the eight passenger and thirty-two freights per day. Persons are unidentified.

Southern Railway Depot at Clinton, Tennessee. About 1914. Persons not identified.

The Oliver Springs Hotel in Oliver Springs, 1895. With eight mineral springs on the grounds, it was a popular resort hotel.

U.S. Government Distillery No. 200, Second District, Tennessee. From left are Ord Yates, holding a testing cup; Niga Green with a mash bucket; George W. Lovely with sacks; Milton Blankenship with a jug; and Brock Foust on Old John Mule. Date about 1898. The distillery was located in Lovely City in Anderson County, believed to be the smallest incorporated town in Tennessee, with 17 qualified voters.

Lee Viles, Special Engineer, in the engine room of the tug vessel, the "Clinton," which was a familiar sight from the wharf at Clinton in the early 1900s. Picture taken in 1912, when hundreds of rafts of logs were brought down Clinch River at high tide.

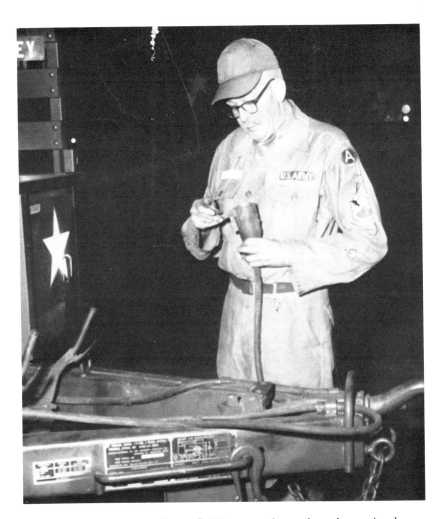

SFC James Harve McCoy of Clinton, who, when he retired was the oldest enlisted man in the U.S. Army. He devoted 46 years of his life to the army. In 1963 two generals told the Sergeant he had to retire and could not re-enlist, but they were wrong. A check of his records showed that he had secured a waiver—signed by Gen. Maxwell D. Taylor.

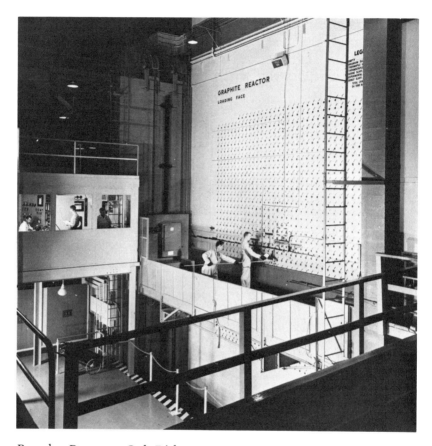

Breeder Reactor, Oak Ridge, now on National Register of Historic Places. *Picture courtesy Office of Public Information, Oak Ridge Operations, U. S. Dept. of Energy.*

Daniel Arthur Rehabilitation Center, Oak Ridge. Left to right: Jessie Thomason; Steve Brody, director of the center; Sheila Coin; Misti Allison; Mrs. Paul Bostic, teacher.

Clinton Community Center, dedicated July 9, 1978.

Byron H. Hale, mayor; Mrs. Joel (Patsy) Meredith, recorder; Charles Seivers, city administrator.

Suggested Readings

The author is currently compiling a comprehensive volume on the history of Anderson County, to be published at a later date.

Anderson County Official Records. 1801-1979.

Burnett, J. J. *Sketches of Tennessee's Pioneer Baptist Preachers, 1775-1875, Volume I.* Nashville, 1919. A history of the beginning of the several associations in the state. One hundred years of Baptist effort and achievement in Tennessee, including sketches of several early Baptist ministers in Anderson County.

Caldwell, Joshua. *Sketches of the Bench and Bar of Tennessee.* Knoxville, 1888. Beginning with the Watauga Association, gives much information about early courts, judges and lawyers riding the circuit, and general background information.

Campbell, T. J. *The Upper Tennessee.* Chattanooga, 1932. Contains records of river operations on the Tennessee River and its tributaries, over a period of 150 years. Several references to Clinch River.

Creekmore, Pollyanna. *Early East Tennessee Taxpayers, I, Anderson County.* Knoxville, 1951. The East Tennessee Historical Society's Publications, No. 23.

Daniels, Jonathan. *A Southerner Discovers the South.* New York, 1938. Two chapters about Norris Dam, the town of Norris, and an interview with David Lilienthal.

Duffus, R. L. *The Valley and its People,* a portrait of TVA. New York, 1944. Interesting information about Norris Dam and other dams built by TVA, with many illustrations.

Groueff, Stephane. *Manhattan Project, The Untold Story of the Making of the Atomic Bomb.* Boston, 1967. A history of the actual building of the bomb, described by the author as "the greatest single achievement of organized effort in history."

Haywood, John. *The Natural and Aboriginal History of Tennessee.* Reprinted, Jackson, 1959, edited by Mary U. Rothrock. Original printed in 1823.

Herr, Kincaid. *Louisville & Nashville Railroad, 1850-1953.* Lousiville, 1964. Information about bringing the line through Anderson County and building of the Dossett tunnel is contained in this book.

Hutson, A. C., Jr. *The Coal Miner's Insurrection of 1891 in Anderson County, Tennessee.* Knoxville, 1935. East Tennessee Historical Society's Publications, No. 7.

_____. *The Overthrow of the Convict Lease System in Tennessee.* Knoxville, 1936. East Tennessee Historical Society's Publications, No. 8.

Lewis, Ronald L. *Race and the United Mine Workers in Tennessee.* Nashville, 1977. Consists largely of selected letters of William R. Riley, a black Union organizer in East Tennessee in the 1890s. His letters contain several references to and incidents in Coal Creek and Briceville in Anderson County. Tennessee Historical Quarterly, Winter 1977.

Lilienthal, David E. *Journals of David E. Lilienthal,* Volumes I and II. New York, 1964.

Morris, Eastin. *The Tennessee Gazeteer.* Nashville, 1834. A topographical dictionary, also containing a description of counties, towns, villages, post offices, rivers, creeks, mountains, and valleys.

Ramsey, Dr. J. G. M. *Autobiography and Letters.* Nashville, 1954. Edited by William B. Hesseltine. Tennessee Historical Society publication.

Richardson, Frank. *From Sunrise to Sunset.* Bristol, 1910. Reminiscences about Methodism in the Clinton Circuit in the 1850s; also his association with some Anderson County men during the Civil War.

Robinson, George C. *The Oak Ridge Story.* Kingsport, 1950. The saga of a people who share in history; the first chapter being the legend of John Hendrix, who many years ago predicted the Oak Ridge of today.

Thompson, Marilou Bonham. *Abiding Appalachia: where mountain and atom meet.* St. Luke's Press, Memphis, 1978. Cherokee legend of Little Deer is fused through poetry with the legend of John Hendrix and the development of the nuclear age.

Index

Abbott, James, 22
Academies, 27-28, 39, 53, 58-59
Adkins, Elijah, 56
Agriculture, early, 23-25; 90-92;
   agricultural extension service, 73-74
Allred, Nora, 62
Alpine, Glen, 71
Altum, Charles, 38
Ambulance service, county, 90
American Carbide & Carbon Company, 85
American Federation of Hosiery Workers,
   Clinton branch, 62
American Legion Auxiliary, 74
American Legion Post, 74, 95
American Red Cross, 72, 80
Amerine, H. G., 75
Anderson, C. G., 18
Anderson County, agent, 73-74; board of
   education, 71; board of realtors, 90-92;
   chairmen, 59-60, 62-68; circuit court
   clerks, 101; clerks & masters, 100;
   commissioners, 89, 102; Company 6th
   Volunteer Infantry, 58; courts, 16, 23,
   27-28, 38, 70, 89; court clerks, 100-101;
   courthouse, 20, 35, 59-60; Court of
   Pleas and Quarter Sessions, 20-21;
   creation of, 13-16; district attorney
   generals, 102-103; early life in, 29-32;
   exemption board, 71; extension service,
   73; fair, 89; formation of, 19-23;
   gubernatorial election (1802), 21;
   judges, 58, 62, 65, 68, 102; justices,
   20-21, 52; seat, 18, 22, 28; officials,
   early, 20-21, 23, 89, 99, 103; park, 89,
   93; population, 102; pound, 22; register
   of deeds, 101; school superintendents,
   101-102; sheriffs, 99-100; social facilities
   and services, 88-90; utility board, 90
Anderson, Margaret, 97
Anderson County News, 61-62, 71, 98
Anderson County Savings Bank, 54
Anderson, David, 18
Anderson, Joseph, descendants of, 18
Andersonville, 22, 37, 41, 52-53, 59,
   69-70, 90; Institute, 53; prison, 42.
Andrews, Forest, 45
Animals, branding of, 23-24
Armstrong, John, 22
Arthur, S. L., 56
Ashlock, Reuben, 38

Ashurst, J. M., 36
Asmond, A. S., 74
Atomic Chain Reactor, 85
Atomic bomb, 85
Attorneys, early 27, 56, 75; attorney
   generals, 102-103; bar association, 93
Authors, local, 97-98
Automobile dealerships, first, 75-76
Avery, Peter, 21

Bailey, James M., 69
Bailey, Wiley, 38
Baker, W. E., 56
Ballard, John, 35
Banks, early, 51, 54, 93; during Civil War,
   47
Baptist, 7, 28-29, 39-40, 53, 59
Barton, Hugh, 28
Baxter, William, 38
Bean, D. B., 45
Beaver Creek, 28
Beech Grove, 76
Bennett, John, 38
Bennett, William, 38
Bessemer Coal, Iron and Land
   Company, 72
Bicentennial projects, 90
Big Mountain Mine, 48
Big Valley Academy, 59
Big Valley Road, 24
Bissell, A. K., 85
Black Diamond Coal Company, 45
Black, James H., 38
Black, John, 36
Black, Sam, 56
Bledsoe County, 26
Blount County, 26
Blount, William, 7, 15
Boating, 25, 51, 92-93
Boone, Daniel, 6
Borum, Luther, 70
Bowden, John, 61
Bowling, A. H., 45
Bowling, Caswell, 36
Bowling, Joel, 54
Braden, Beulah Brummett, 97
Branding, of animals, 23
Bryan, Ebenezer, 21
Brazelton, Isaac, 22
Breiver, Alberta and Carson, 97

124   *Tennessee County History Series*

Katherine Baker Hoskins was born June 25, 1908, in Clinton, Tennessee, where she received her formal education. She was employed by Magnet Mills, Inc., for 25 years as secretary to the president and assistant to the personnel director. While she worked in the personnel department, she served as editor of *The Magnet,* the mill's employee publication. For six years during this time, she was a member of the National Board of Directors of the American Association of Industrial Editors. She also served as president of the Appalachian Industrial Editors Association for four years and edited the East Tennessee Historical Society Quarterly, *Echoes,* for two years. During the early 1940s, she filled a two-year term as Anderson County Circuit Court Clerk. In 1978 Mrs. Hoskins retired as Director of Budgets and Accounts for Anderson County, a position she had held since 1966. For the past five years she has written the historical column for the *Clinton Courier News.*

She is the wife of the late Gomer D. Hoskins, who was a title attorney for TVA. Mrs. Hoskins has three children, Clyde B. Hoskins, Susan Hoskins Whitehead, and Martha Hoskins Frye. A fourth child, Gomer Hoskins, Jr., was killed in Vietnam in 1967.

Mrs. Hoskins has been active in the Clinton Business and Professional Women's Club, St. Mark's Methodist Church, the Order of Amaranth, the Anderson County Library Board, and the Board of Directors of the Clinton Chamber of Commerce. She also served on the Board of Directors for the Clinch-Powell Regional Library.